PRAISE FOR BILL RATNER

D1009078

"Lucid and thought-provoking,"

—Jane Claire, Barnes & Noble

"In a world that bombards and seduces us with technology and the never-ending attraction of yet another fancy device, Bill Ratner offers that rare and old-fashioned thing that no hand-held device will ever make obsolete: a good old-fashioned story, of a father who makes his life in media, confronted by the dangers of too much television and too many computers. And his wise decision to unplug.

"Ratner offers wise and sober words (and sometimes funny ones) on an issue that has transformed our society, along with a valuable antidote for getting back to what matters most: human relationships."

—Joyce Maynard, author of *Labor Day*

"More than just the premier voice-over talent in Hollywood today, Ratner writes with the subtlety and texture worthy of a literary fiction master."

—Brad Schreiber, *Huffington Post*

"From kindergartner entranced with disembodied voices on TV and radio . . . to voiceover stardom and family man, . . . Bill Ratner's life keeps bursting the confines of the ordinary . . ."

—Anita Frankel, Psychologist

"It's a great, sweet, well-told story with humor, heart, nuance, and depth."

—Lea Thau, Independent Producers Project/KCRW Radio, Los Angeles

"Bill Ratner has been involved in the industry for most of his life, coming from a home where his dad was an ad executive for General Mills and helped personify the image of Betty Crocker for the world. Ratner has a way of bringing those images in his head into perfect focus."

—Bob Leggett, *The Examiner*

"Bill Ratner is one of the most enjoyable storytellers in Los Angeles."

—Gary Buchler, Storytelling Producer, TheMoth.org

"High-caliber storyteller."

—L. J. Williamson, *LA Weekly*

"The behind-the-scenes stories of his life as a big-time announcer are lots of fun, but I found the family scenes most affecting. . . . A fascinating life journey, told by a master storyteller. . . ."

—Beau Weaver, SpokenWord.com

"He expertly guides us on a journey through not just his own life, but the kind of life that many in the creative and entertainment fields will recognize: early infatuation with all manner of media . . . and finally, pondering the sublime mysteries of life and human existence itself. . ."

—Joel Bellman, of Los Angeles County Board of Supervisors

PARENTING

FOR THE

DIGITAL

AGE

PARENTING

FOR THE

DIGITAL AGE

THE TRUTH BEHIND MEDIA'S EFFECT ON
CHILDREN, AND WHAT TO DO ABOUT IT

BILL RATNER

Published by Familius LLC, www.familius.com

Familius books are available at special discounts for bulk purchases for sales promotions, family or corporate use. Special editions, including personalized covers, excerpts of existing books, or books with corporate logos, can be created in large quantities for special needs. For more information, contact Premium Sales at 559-876-2170 or email specialmarkets@familius.com

Library of Congress Catalog-in-Publication Data

2014952333

pISBN 978-1-939629-05-0
eISBN 978-1-939629-00-5

Printed in the United States of America

Edited by Brooke Jorden
Cover design by David Miles
Book design by Maggie Wickes

10 9 8 7 6 5 4 3 2 1

First Edition

CONTENTS

ACKNOWLEDGMENTS

I owe a tremendous debt of gratitude to the principal of Los Angeles' Allesandro Elementary School, Lynn Andrews, who for over twenty years has welcomed me into his school where many of my ideas about children, technology, and the media were formed, and to his talented team of teachers, including Willi Matsamura and Carolyn Naylor.

I'm grateful to Familius' Michele Robbins, who gave me the idea for this book, and to storyteller Susan O'Halloran for giving us a space where it could develop. Thanks to my Uncle Gerry, who has passed down the family treasure trove of stories.

Thanks to my dear friends Fred Silverman, Roberta Alexandra, Sea Glassman, Mila DaRosa, Sean Carter, Adele Robbins, interviewees Larry Brooks, Anna Marie Piersimoni, Marc Brooks, Nina Brooks, Peter Weich, Bridget Weich, Stefan Weich, Sonja Weich, Sara Waters, Mary MacDonald-Lewis, Chris Anthony-Lansdowne, my teachers Aaron Henne, Erin Jourdan, Emily Rapp, David Ulin, Jill Essbaum, Chuck Evered, Kate Anger, and my editor, Brooke Jorden, for all their help.

Thanks to Richard Herman and Roy and Maggie Nevitt of Windsor Mountain International and to my fellow storytellers at The Moth Storytelling for nurturing my stories.

Thanks to my wife, Aleka, and my daughters, Arianna and Miranda, for their love, creativity, and patience. And finally to my parents and my brother, Pete, for their time, their love, and wisdom, without which none of this would be possible.

FOREWORD

I first met author Bill Ratner on a sunny summer day in rural New Hampshire, when Bill arrived with his wife and daughter for a visit to the kids' camp I founded in 1961—Interlocken International, now called Windsor Mountain International. At age four months, Bill's daughter Arianna was much too young to be a camper. Our camp kids were between nine and thirteen years old. But Bill and his young family had come to find out what we were doing deep in the woods with over two hundred kids and grownups from around the world who had come to learn, explore, and have fun together.

The skillset that Bill brought to camp that summer set us on a course that endures to this day. Bill is a storyteller, and I took every opportunity to put Bill to work at camp, telling stories at morning meeting, in our theater classes, and at night around the campfire. Storytelling is great fun, but it is also the way mankind has passed on its collective wisdom from generation to generation. Storytelling is the frame through which we see our world. And Bill is a master storyteller. His kids became campers, he returned year after year, and as his reputation grew, residents of nearby towns would come to Interlocken on Festival Eve just to hear Bill's many tales told around the blazing campfire.

We referred to life at camp as "Life in the Bubble"—the gentle, organized, creative, and supportive atmosphere that comprised camp life at Interlocken. What didn't belong in the bubble were behaviors and technologies that distracted campers from our daily goals: to learn new things, make new friends, and flourish in a safe, semi-wilderness environment. With the advent of PlayStation, Nintendo, Xbox, smart phones, and tablets, we faced an onslaught of technology arriving at camp with the kids every summer. But we had rules:

no electronic games, no cellphones. In case of emergency, of course, a child could speak with his or her parents, but we found over the years that cellphones and gaming platforms were not only an unnecessary distraction for kids, but also an obstacle to fully experiencing the rich, creative life at camp.

So, in as gentle a manner as possible, having warned families in advance, we stored kids' phones and electronic games for the duration of their stay at camp. Was there push-back? Of course. Kids are habituated to answering every text and playing every game on their device. Did their resistance disappear? Yes. Within minutes of arrival, kids were doing what kids do—making friends, tossing a Frisbee, singing songs, going for a swim, and settling in to a technology-free life at camp.

This book is an essential tool for every parent and caregiver. It tells the story of how and why digital technology has crept so far into our lives, how its overuse affects children, and how to control it. This book is filled with stories, both fun and intriguing. Bill came from an advertising family and has worked in the Hollywood entertainment business most of his adult life, so he has had a bird's-eye view of how the makers of children's media can lure families into buying what they don't need and spending time in front of screens that could otherwise be spent more happily.

I am honored to call Bill my friend. And we still meet up for long chats and walks in the woods of the Northeast. Can we all return to the innocence and beauty of life in rural New England? Probably not, but we can start the conversation with our children and begin to build the framework of a sensibly controlled atmosphere in our homes where digital technology can support a creative, nurturing environment, rather than overrun it. This book is the key to starting down that welcome path.

Richard Herman
Founder and Director Emeritus, Windsor Mountain International

INTRODUCTION

Families have a problem. Our children have too many screens to watch—TVs, phones, tablets, computers, digital video recorders, gaming platforms. And they're spending too much time watching. Like a horde of territorial invaders, the makers of screens, games, and children's programming have descended upon the land with a covetous eye toward our wallets. Children in tow, we head for the hills, hoping to make it to safety. But as in a sci-fi movie, the invaders have placed pods, pads, phones, and monitors into our homes, and we watch warily as our children paw over their new "smart" phones and "smart" TVs, learning faster than we ever did how to operate them. And they settle in, well-prepared for a childhood of couch-surfing. What's wrong with that? There are lots of opinions and studies, but the jury is still out on whether the current generation of children living a "wired" existence will be better or worse off than their non-digital predecessors.

My father, Joe Ratner, was an advertising executive, and he saw it coming. He was a wise, generous parent, and a good storyteller. He taught me the nature of electronic media. He made sure that I was aware at an early age of the mesmerizing power and the primary functions of children's commercial entertainment—to keep you watching and to sell you things. To my father, the children's electronic entertainment business was a game of smoke and mirrors based upon well-planned sales strategies targeting young people. He taught me the rules. And he set limits.

This book is divided into two sections: (1) challenges and (2) solutions. It is a combination personal memoir and parenting guide. In the first section, I go back in time to when children's media was in its formative stages, and I look at how it got here from there. I explore my own childhood, growing up in an advertising household. I investigate why our children's lives today have become so cluttered with entertainment options and how the makers of digital devices and children's electronic entertainment keep our children glued to their screens. Section two offers real-world solutions to a crisis that is reducing our children's quality of life and wasting the most important thing they are given—time.

I use digital devices every day. I am the voice of thousands of movie trailers, TV shows, cartoons, computer games, and commercials. I got my first job in the media business when I was fourteen years old, packing promotional posters into cardboard tubes in the basement of our next-door neighbor. I worked my way through high school as an errand boy for Campbell-Mithun Advertising Agency in Minneapolis. As a child, I had the privilege of looking over my father's shoulder and watching him design advertising campaigns as Managing Editor of *Better Homes & Gardens* magazine and, later, Creative Director for Campbell-Mithun Advertising Agency, and Executive Vice President of Marketing for General Mills, Inc.

"This is advertising, kid. This is how we keep products hopping off the shelves." This was one of the many pithy declarations my father made to me about the media as I grew up. I am lucky that he took an interest in how I perceived advertising and electronic entertainment. Not only did he help me get where I am today, but he also helped me create an open dialogue with my children about what they encounter online and on TV, and how they interact with social media, computer games, and the plethora of devices available to them. In our house, in collaboration with our children, my wife and I control the multi-screen environment.

I have two important responsibilities—I am an entertainment professional and a parent. My experience in the world of children's media and its array of delivery systems has made me a better and more conscientious parent. I am not a whistle-blower. I simply have stories to tell. And by sharing with you my experiences working with electronic media and parenting in the digital age, I intend to help you and your family better understand the "wired" world and how to manage it, rather than let it manage you. As for giving advice to you about exactly how to slap controls on the viewing/gaming/social media/web-surfing habits of your kids, part of me wants to quote the rear bumper sticker on police cars: "Just say no," (or as comedian Emily Levine says, "Just say no, *thank you*."). But for families, this issue is far more complex.

The good news is parents have a wide range of options, strategies, and tactics they can use to moderate the effects on their children of too many devices and too much media. Most importantly, we'll discuss how you can have a direct, ongoing dialogue with your children which is vital to their development as responsible, happy, empathic, and productive human beings. I urge families to talk openly with each other about the problems associated with excessive screen time. Having conversations with your children is always better than silence. And we'll address how to set limits and how to stick with them. You'll read interviews with families and their children and find out how they survive the digital onslaught.

Parents are also talking directly to the media marketplace about these issues. There is a long history in America of parents banding together to implement strategies to protect their children from the media. Parents can be a powerful and effective public voice affecting not only legislation but also the behavior of corporate media. It's amazing what a little organizing can do. Media companies want your business, and they listen when you're upset.

This book grew out of a workshop I took from Chicago storyteller Susan O'Halloran, "Teaching without Preaching," at the Timpanogos Storytelling Festival in Provo, Utah, where folklorists, librarians, teachers, parents, students, storytellers, and story-fanciers gather annually for a three-day weekend to study with and listen to professional storytellers from all over the world. In Susan O'Halloran's workshop, she told us, "Each one of you is about to create something that comes from your heart, a project you believe in. It might be an idea for a class you can teach or a book for young readers. Whatever it is, it will be uniquely yours. And with the help of your workshop partner, you are going to create it right here, right now."

I stared at my desk. What would I create? For a moment, I thought the most constructive thing I could create would be a plan for spring cleaning of my office back in Los Angeles. But there wouldn't be much to talk about with my workshop partner, Michele Robbins, besides the relative merits of the broom versus the vacuum cleaner. I assumed Michele was a graduate student. She turned out to be a middle-aged publisher and mother of nine children. Who knew that parenting could keep you looking so young? Throughout Susan O'Halloran's workshop, Michele and I tossed ideas back and forth. Since I work in the media, I figured the most logical thing for me to create would be media related. My mind drifted back to when I first started working in television as a cartoon voice actor, and it hit me—I am part of the problem. The voice acting roles I play in children's television shows are a significant lure used to get children to watch . . . and buy. So I used the morning to review and revise my volunteer program I perform in schools, "TV Cartoon Scandals: Media Awareness for Children."

In the following chapters, I discuss my experiences as a parent, a child of the media, an educator, and a veteran insider from the world of television and new media. I hope these stories and suggestions will help you understand how we got where we are; why and how the makers of children's TV programs, websites, software, and devices do what they do; and how you can be better prepared to parent for the digital age.

PART I
CHALLENGES

Today's world is full of challenges for families. Children are watching repurposed TV shows and uncensored advertisements on digital devices—large and small. They surf websites of every nature imaginable and play an endless array of computer games. Putting an innocent-looking "smart" phone in the hands of a toddler is a powerful lure for parents. Your child appears totally absorbed, and you can rest. So easy, so freeing. . . . So what's the problem? No one is exactly sure.

Psychologists and educators say the learned behaviors that make a child human and allow him to negotiate our complex world might be stunted by too much screen time at an early age. Does this make you worry? Where did all this technology come from? Are the makers of these devices targeting your child?

These are some of the questions I attempt to answer in this book. In order for us to understand today's world of digital technology we need to go back in time to an era that was technologically less complex, but certainly no more innocent. By understanding the beginnings of children's media and technology, I intend to help you come up with a simple strategy, so that you can have the family life that you desire.

CHAPTER ONE

THE TV BROKE, DADDY

As quietly as possible, I snuck down the basement stairs, reached into the secret place in the wall, and threw the switch.

"The TV broke, Daddy," said my four-year-old daughter Arianna in the saddest little voice as she stood in the middle of our family room in front of the television set.

"Oh, no, really?" I said as I emerged from the basement. I responded in as comforting a parental tone as I could muster as my four-year-old frantically punched the on/off button on the TV in our family room.

"Is it really broken?" my wife asked with the faintest sound of relief.

I whispered, "It's not broken."

"It's not broken?" echoed my four-year-old, tugging at her dance tutu.

"Uh, it is," I stammered. "Honey, I'm so sorry, but it looks like the TV is broken. Daddy will try and fix it, but if I can't, we'll have to call the TV repairman—"

"—and that could take weeks," said my wife heading back into the kitchen, a sly smile on her lips.

My wife was well aware of my devious secret. She had been in on the planning. But it was growing increasingly difficult for me to extricate myself from the lie I had concocted for the benefit of my children—a lie that involved hiring an electrician to alter the electric circuits in our house so that we could create mysterious power outages at the entertainment center in our family room with a secret switch in the basement.

In a desperate attempt to stem the merciless loss of time that my four-year-old had begun to spend sitting in front of an electronic screen of one sort or another, we decided to have a secret cutoff switch installed. With the flick of a switch, I could cut off power to our TV monitor, our DVD player, VHS player, computer, video game platform, and the DVR. Only my wife and I knew of the switch's existence. This, of course, didn't address the later issue of gathering up cell phones. We would conduct that chore like a pickpocket grabs your wallet—we simply took them.

I had gotten the idea for the cutoff switch from my father-in-law, Jack. When my wife was a child in the fourth grade, she began to exhibit problems with reading. Her older sister, Laurie, was not an enthusiastic reader either. Jack was alarmed. He was a media insider; he sold commercial air time for TV stations. And he was a voracious reader—anything he could get his hands on, from history to current events. But the very thing that put food on his family's dinner table—television—appeared to be retarding the development of his own children's reading habits. He surmised that they were watching too much TV. So, one night, under cover of darkness, Jack snuck into the living room, pried open the back of their RCA Victor television set, removed a handful of vacuum tubes, and hid them away in the broom closet.

The next day, the inevitable question came, "Daddy, what happened to the TV?"

"Gosh, kids, looks like we'll have to call the TV repairman."

The TV repairman never came. Seven years went by. Jack's

daughters pestered him about the "broken" TV set. But in the meantime, they became a family of readers. Today, my wife is grateful to her father for the decision he made to leave their television set "broken." She is a voracious reader like her father.

But I kept wondering if this was the best way to deal with the problem of how my child spent her time. I certainly felt powerful when I threw the switch in the basement and feigned ignorance as to why all the screens in the family room suddenly went dark. Was I afraid to confront my own daughter with what my wife and I both firmly believed—that she had begun to spend way too much time sitting passively in front of an electronic screen? Was I afraid of the resistance and pushback I would get when I tried to explain to her that I believe that too much screen time robs her of a precious, irreplaceable commodity in her life that she will never get back—time? Time that, in order for her to become a fully-formed, communicative, well-rounded human being, should be spent relating with family and friends, learning to read, and using verbal, social, and emotional skills of negotiation, compromise, and fair play—skills that can only be learned face-to-face. And would there be time for just playing—lying in the grass staring at the sky, imagining, dreaming?

When my daughter Arianna turned five, she witnessed a spirited conversation between her friends at kindergarten about the latest TV episode of *Teenage Mutant Ninja Turtles*. When she got home she asked, "Daddy, how come you won't let me watch *Ninja Turtles*?"

I gulped nervously and scrambled for a reason to give her other than my gut feeling about the possible results of letting her watch too much TV. Was I being too cautious? After all, my parents let me watch TV as a kid, but there were far fewer choices for young viewers back then. The only screen we had in our house was a black-and-white television set, and children's programming accounted for a much smaller proportion of the overall diet of TV shows.

The *Teenage Mutant Ninja Turtles* TV cartoon series was born in 1987, the same year as my daughter, and by the time she entered preschool, *Teenage Mutant Ninja Turtles* merchandise—from Pez dispensers to skateboards, breakfast cereal, video games, school supplies, linens, towels, cameras, and even toy shaving kits—flew off the shelves featuring images of Leonardo, Michelangelo, Donatello, Rafael, and the rest of the characters in the show.

The movie *Teenage Mutant Ninja Turtles II: The Secret of the Ooze*, had just been released in theaters. So, as an attempt to divert my preschooler's attention away from her question of "Why won't you let me watch *The Turtles* on TV?" I offered to take her to the movie.

Her eyes widened in unbridled excitement. "Yeah, can we?"

Going to a film in a movie theater is a more controllable experience than watching television at home. I could schedule a trip to the multiplex and discuss the movie with her in the car on the way home, leaving the violence and base silliness of the film behind at the movie theater. But our TV set lurked ever-present inside our house, and at any time my child might demand, "I want to watch TV."

I wasn't sure how to answer her question, "Why can't I watch TV?" Studies show that there are negative effects on children from spending too many hours in front of an electronic screen, including reduced attention span, increased social fears, and most importantly, time lost from school work, reading, and social interaction with peers and family. It is my belief that the more time children can spend on the swings in the yard with friends, drawing with finger paints, tossing a Frisbee, listening to their mom and dad read stories aloud—engaging in live activities with fellow humans rather than in front of an electronic screen—the better off they'll be.

UCLA neuroscientist Dr. Gary Small author of *iBrain: Surviving the Technological Alteration of the Modern Mind*, writes, "The downside of such immersion in technological devices is that [children are] not having conversations, looking people in the eye, or noticing verbal cues. These are important 'technologies,' so to speak, that have evolved over centuries and are tremendously powerful."[1]

On my first day as a freshman Journalism student at Michigan

State University, my professor, a wizened old newspaper man from the *Detroit Free Press*, stood before the class and said, "Behind every story are the Five W's and the H." He listed these questions on the board.

- What happened?
- Why did it happen?
- When did it happen?
- Where did it happen?
- Who was there?
- How did it happen?

When I ponder the problems children face in the new world of electronic media, I find myself asking:

- What are we dealing with here?
- Why do we feel helpless?
- When did it all go wrong?
- Where do we go for help?
- Who's in charge here?
- How do we deal with it?

Current data shows that between ages two and eighteen American kids spend over six of their waking hours every day staring at an electronic screen. Watching TV accounts for over half of that time.[2] Only a small fraction of this screen time is spent doing homework. The rest of their time is spent gaming, texting, instant messaging, emailing, and navigating an ever-widening stream of social media sites: Facebook, Twitter, Instagram, Snapchat, etc.—the list grows every day. Studies show that kids in first-world countries are growing obese, and even the academic test scores of our highest young achievers are falling. Our kids are pigging out on screen time.

When my eldest daughter was two years old, our television set broke, so we replaced it. When we unboxed the new monitor, my daughter stared at our new TV as if she were seeing the fathomless depths of the ocean for the first time. I decided to conduct an experiment. I had heard that toddlers do not naturally gravitate to watching TV, that when they aren't exploring the physical world with their busy hands and mouths, they are predisposed to seek attention from fellow humans and to ignore TV. A television screen is two-dimensional—mainly talking heads and noise.

But parents know that one way to get some free time away from their children is to try and get them to accept a parental substitute—the "electronic babysitter."[3] But it turns out that it does take some effort to get your child to let go of your pants leg and sit quietly in front of the TV set. A small child is action-oriented, prone to crawling, grabbing, testing—not sitting still. In order to get a toddler hooked on TV, a parent must sit down with the child repeatedly and habituate them to the unnatural activity of sitting quietly and watching an electronic screen. But once that step is taken, once the parent commits his child to screen time, as with anything addictive, it's difficult to go back.

I wanted to prove my theorem that a toddler has a natural resistance to watching TV. So, as my two-year-old daughter stared at our new television monitor, I handed her the remote and demonstrated how to use the channel-changing buttons. She quickly took charge, and as she pushed the buttons over and over, the screen displayed newscasters, soap opera actors, commercial pitchmen—all frantically moving their lips and making noise. This bored my daughter, and she pushed the button faster and faster until the screen was a blur of talking heads. (We have satellite TV with lots of channels, so there was a lot of button pushing to do.) She hesitated only at the channels dedicated to children's programming, but even these seemed to bore her. And after a minute or so of channel surfing, she dropped the remote on the floor and resumed playing with her dolls. Was my child unique? Was she TV resistant? Had we somehow dodged a bullet?

Unfortunately we hadn't. The fusillade was coming. Soon our child would be besieged by an immense offering of programming aimed exclusively at children on both TV and the internet—ABC Family, Animal Planet, BabyFirst TV, Boomerang, Cartoon Network, Disney

Channels, Nickelodeon, etc. And soon our daughter would be asking for an iPhone, an iPad, a Gameboy, and a laptop computer.

As parents, we face a complex and ever-changing set of questions about our children's screen time.

- How much screen time is too much?
- How does screen time affect a child?
- How do you talk with a child about screen time?

I have always chosen to limit my children's screen time in order to help them pursue more active and social activities. But, as LaVar Burton from the PBS TV show *Reading Rainbow* used to say, "You don't have to take my word for it."

The National Association of Broadcasters (NAB) Television Code reads:

> Television and all who participate in it are jointly account-able to the American public for respect for the special needs of children, for community responsibility, for the advance-ment of education and culture, for the acceptability of the program materials chosen, for decency and decorum in production, and for propriety in advertising.

Do television programmers adhere to this lofty-sounding credo?

At an NAB meeting in Washington, DC, Newton Minow, Chair-man of the Federal Communications Commission (FCC), told a gathering of top TV executives:

> When television is bad, nothing is worse. . . . Sit down in front of your television set . . . and stay there, for a day, without a book, without a magazine, without a newspaper, without a profit and loss sheet or a rating book to distract you. Keep your eyes glued to that set. . . . I can assure you that what you will observe is a vast wasteland, . . . a procession of game shows, formula comedies about totally unbe-lievable families, blood and thunder, mayhem, violence, sadism, murder, private eyes, gangsters, more violence, and

cartoons. And endlessly, commercials—many screaming, cajoling, and offending. And most of all, boredom. True, you'll see a few things you will enjoy. But they will be very, very few. And if you think I exaggerate, I only ask you to try it. . . . Is there one person in this room who claims that broadcasting can't do better?[4]

This speech could have easily been given this year. But the Chairman of the FCC spoke these words on May 9, 1961, during the decline of the so-called Golden Age of Television, an era which is celebrated today for its quality dramatic programming and innovative news shows—a time when the only electronic media platform parents had to worry about was television. Today, children are watching television programming on smart phones, smart TVs, tablets, and computers. Plus they are gaming, web-surfing, and texting. And media experts are alarmed.

Newsweek/Daily Beast writer Tony Dokoupil warns, "The current incarnation of the Internet—portable, social, accelerated, and all-pervasive—may be making us not just dumber or lonelier, but more depressed and anxious, prone to obsessive-compulsive and attention-deficit disorders, even outright psychotic. Our digitized minds can scan like those of drug addicts, and normal people are breaking down in sad and seemingly new ways."[5]

KidsHealth.org says, "The first two years of life are considered a critical time for brain development. TV and other electronic media can get in the way of exploring, playing, and interacting with parents and others, which encourages learning and healthy physical and social development."[6]

Francisca Theresia of Monterey Peninsula College writes, "In research made by the American Psychological Association (APA), it is stated that, 'The more children watch violence on TV, the more fearful and distrustful they become of the world.' According to a study made by the University of Pennsylvania, 'Excessive exposure to television made children passive and unresponsive to their surroundings.'"[7]

Imagine, for a moment, your child on a gentle bicycle ride down a tree-lined lane, a lazy afternoon spent counting frogs at the edge of a pond, and in the distance Mom is on the back porch ringing the dinner bell, calling your child's name. And after supper, a cozy evening is spent by the fire, the family curled together up with a good book. Is this a naïve dream from the irretrievable past? With proper parental controls, all this can be experienced by twenty-first century children, even as they are besieged by an endless array of electronic media platforms that, uncontrolled, cause them to spend way too much time in front of an electronic screen designed to win their eyeballs and keep them—forever.

Daniel Goleman reports in *The New York Times*, "Jerome Singer, a psychologist at Yale University, holds that people who watch too much television from childhood grow up with a deprived fantasy life. For them, watching television substitutes for their own imagination."[8]

Aside from our own warm and fuzzy memories of our favorite animated movie or children's TV show, do we really trust the mammoth, cash-rich media corporations that lure our children's eyeballs to their screens like Apple, Microsoft, Amazon, and YouTube? Computers, smart phones, and tablets can help us schedule our time, catch up on the latest news, communicate with friends and family, and generally amuse us. And they can serve as study aids for both adults and children. But uncontrolled, electronic media platforms can take over a child's life and substitute programming for imagination, icons for thoughts, and pre-scripted scenarios and endless dramas created by total strangers for real life.

Media outlets and advertisers are targeting younger and younger audiences. At a Sunday afternoon brunch in a friend's backyard, I had a spirited argument with my hosts about allowing their twelve-year-old daughter to subscribe to a popular teen magazine and its website. My daughter was also twelve.

"These are young girls," I warned. "This is a magazine for older teens whose priorities are very different from a twelve-year-old's."

"They're tweens," her father responded. "They're in between childhood and being a teen."

In my view, this still didn't make our daughters old enough to start thinking about the things teen magazines put before their audiences. Is it appropriate for a twelve-year-old girl to be on a website or read a magazine where she's asked, "What's your summer love dare?" Or, "Sex Q&A: Why won't he make a move?" Or "Who's your One Direction love match?"

I don't feel that these questions (taken from actual teen magazine sites), if they are to be asked at all, should be asked of a twelve-year-old girl.

The retail clothing industry comes up with ever-more sophisticated ways to sell its products, and it has focused its sights on younger and younger children. The tween has become a very lucrative target for advertisers. Marketing directly to the tween girl has earned billions of dollars for Forever 21, H&M, TJ Maxx, etc., and the list grows every year.

With the onslaught of young persons' social media sites, smart phone apps, computer games, magazines, and television shows, parents can feel helpless. To control multiple screens, we can subscribe to the parental control features offered by our cable TV provider. We can use software to limit the kinds of websites our children can visit online. We can even purchase computer spyware to monitor our children's online activity. But what about when our kids are at the neighbors' house or in the library or on their smart phones away from home? Trying to apply all of these controls is a bit like playing whack-a-mole at the county fair. You knock one down its hole, and another one pops right up. My suggestion is to talk directly with your kids. Discuss the problem, make the rules, and stick to them.

In our family, the hardest part of childrearing has been enduring the inevitable rejection and anger that our children throw at us when they don't get their way (when we take away the smart phone for an evening, when we don't allow websurfing during homework, etc.) I never felt more like a hangman/executioner than on the nights when I had to take my daughters' cellphones away and shove them in my sock drawer in order for the kids to get started on their homework.

Psychologists say that when our children shout their demands and complaints at us, they are rehearsing to get their way in the world. Parents are the easiest and safest targets for them to practice on. Will we cover our ears, or will we take the opportunity to teach, guide, and protect?

CHAPTER TWO

HOW WE CAME TO THIS

I played the voice of "Flint" in the original Hasbro TV cartoon series, *G.I. Joe: A Real American Hero*. "Flint" also made special appearances in Cartoon Network's *Robot Chicken* and Fox TV's *Family Guy*. Right after Hasbro, Inc., started producing *G.I. Joe* in 1982, action figures of my character, Flint, and other *G.I. Joe* characters began popping up on store shelves faster and in greater numbers than ever before in the history of toy merchandising. Something had changed in the American toy marketplace, but only TV advertisers, Washington insiders, and a few parent media watchdog groups appeared to be aware of the change.

In 1982, for the first time since television broadcasting regulations were drafted in the 1930s, the Federal Communications Commission (FCC) and the Federal Trade Commission (FTC) relaxed the rules that governed advertising within children's TV programs. The Reagan Administration, feeling residual pressure from the 1980 recession and the Mideast oil crisis, wanted to bring some relief to advertisers and give the economy a boost. As a result, by 1984, US regulators had removed many of the restrictions regarding the placement of promotional content within children's television programming. Plus, Hasbro figured out a way around the rules that remained by advertising the *G.I. Joe* comic book on TV, and not the action figures themselves. The immediate results were:

- A dramatic increase in the quantity of TV ads aimed specifically at children.[9]
- An uptick in child-consumerism and obesity amongst children.[10]
- A boost in toy merchandisers' stock prices.[11]
- An alarming rise in the number of hours children spent in front of TV screens.[12]

Despite the risks to children, advertisers and TV networks were ecstatic over the rule changes. It meant more ways to sell products and more revenue for broadcasters. But parent watchdog groups were alarmed. Educators, media experts, and mental health professionals have always believed that young TV viewers are different from adults.[13] Children are more susceptible to the manipulative messages inside TV ads, and children age six and under believe that what they see on television is real. A study at Nagoya University in Japan revealed that up until the age of five and a half, children believe that what appears on a TV screen is actually there in the room with them—whether it is an action figure hurtling through space or a delicious-looking candy bar being shoved into a young actor's mouth in a TV commercial.[14]

The TV cartoon episodes I voiced and the commercials I narrated ballyhooed an endless parade of action figures, toy vehicles, and comic books. As a result of the change in the FCC rules and Hasbro's new marketing tactics, kids' TV programs were no longer just amusing childhood diversions; they had become hard-charging, thirty-minute infomercials for toys and action figures. Though I loved having the voiceover work, I began to feel that I was part of the problem.

But wasn't this just innocent kid stuff? As a child, I had tugged on my dad's sleeve in the five-and-dime store and begged for my first pair of Disney Mickey Mouse ears after seeing an episode of *The Mickey Mouse Club* on TV. But back then, the FCC rules were different. In a children's TV show, it was illegal to advertise toys that were based on the characters in the show. If children's TV had been unregulated back then, I would have been watching commercial after commercial and pestering my parents day and night to buy me the action figures I saw advertised in my favorite TV shows. With all that screen time, today, I would be an advertiser's dream come true—and a parent's worst nightmare.

I have often wandered the aisles of my local supermarket with my fingers in my ears, trying to block out the shrill cries of a nearby child begging his parent for a brand-specific product he spotted on the store shelf. Chances are he saw it advertised on TV. Advertising works well on children. But it works only in proportion to the amount of TV they are allowed to watch.

I had a love/hate relationship with television as a child. I was slavishly devoted to certain programs like *Fearless Fosdick*, a police procedural for children performed live with marionettes; *Dragnet*, starring Jack Webb, an LAPD favorite; and *The Ernie Kovacs Show*, where viewers were introduced to a comedic and very grownup world sponsored by Dutch Masters Cigars. As for *Captain Kangaroo*, *Howdy Doody*, and much of children's programming in those days, I was often bored. But despite my boredom, I sat for hours in front of the "idiot box," as my father called it. I spent way too much time watching whatever appeared on the screen. I even watched the TV station test pattern that appeared on the screen before sign-on preceding Saturday morning TV. I spent Saturday mornings and after-school hours staring idly at the television screen until my parents discovered me, bleary-eyed, and rescued me from my TV-induced trance. My dad simply shut off the TV and walked me to the park for a game of catch.

Back in the early 1950s, TV was a novelty, a young medium. But as commercial television matured and nearly every American family bought a set, TV become the object of scrutiny on the part of educators, child-development experts, and parent groups. Despite these concerns, advertisers and tech futurists dreamed of a world where there would be numerous ways for children to view programming and advertising—a world of many screens. And that is what we face now.

Today, in addition to TV, there is gaming, social media, and a myriad of ways to watch TV programs repurposed for the web. What children see advertised online and on TV affects their parents' consuming patterns. Children and teens influence billions of dollars' worth of parental purchases every year.[15] And that is due in great part to the advertising kids see online and on TV. Even many so-called educational TV shows have a very different, very profitable, purpose in mind. Public Broadcasting is proud of its long-running and very successful show *Sesame Street*. But even at PBS, all that glitters is not gold—except when it comes to selling toys.

When PBS launched *Sesame Street* in 1969, the network mailed workbooks to thousands of American families with specific instructions for parents to sit down and watch the show with their children and actively participate in the spelling and arithmetic exercises. Claims were made about the positive effects *Sesame Street* had on children's moods and on their ability to retain concepts of arithmetic and spelling. However, the most-quoted study was conducted by PBS itself. Child viewers' math and spelling test scores did improve with watching *Sesame Street* . . . as long as their parents were actively involved in watching and participating in the program with their kids. Children who watched *Sesame Street* alone, without parents present, showed no improvement in retention of math and spelling concepts. Even when parents followed PBS's instructions and participated in watching, their children lost their edge in math and spelling test scores over lone viewers and non-viewers as they entered elementary school.[16] So, even the vaunted *Sesame Street* turned out to be not much more than pure entertainment. And over the decades, the sale of *Sesame Street* toys has racked up hundreds of millions of dollars in profits.

While it may not teach children to read, *Sesame Street*, along with the flood of commercial children's TV programs and websites, instills in young users a sense of personal ownership, which keeps them watching. Viewers, especially children, often feel that their favorite programs and the tools they use to watch them—their TV, smart phone, laptop, or tablet—are their special friends—theirs and theirs alone to treasure and squeeze pleasure from. "My channel, my website, my iPhone." A sense of ownership is exactly what tech manufacturers and the purveyors of internet and TV programming want young people to feel. In a *Los Angeles Times* article about kids buying items promoted online by celebrities, a thirteen-year-old girl says, "You kind of feel closer to them in a way by owning stuff."[17] Children lovingly treasure their purchases, phones, and tablets, paid for by their parents, but all that merchandise, technology, and programming comes from hugely profitable global communications conglomerates. And it's all about monetizing. The challenge for parents is to find ways to affirm children's self-esteem and their membership in their group of peers while making sure that they know the difference between self-worth and simply owning a smart phone, Gameboy, or t-shirt.

When my oldest daughter was in sixth grade, she and her friends fell in love the Japanese brand of Hello Kitty toys. My daughter and her friends clipped Hello Kitty merchandise to their backpacks, and they traded items at school. This all came crashing down when some kids began stealing Hello Kitty toys from each other, and the school principal imposed a ban on Hello Kitty toys on campus. The parents were relieved, and so were the kids, who had grown weary of the competition and thievery.

While working as an errand boy at Campbell-Mithun Advertising in Minneapolis, I attended a marketing seminar. CEO and founder, Ray Mithun, told his account executives, "The most important part of our job is to create advertising that makes the buyer feel like what he has purchased is the most special thing in the world."

Somewhere in storage most of us have a treasure trove of toys from our childhood that we pledged to give to our children, hoping they will love them as much as we did. Alas, it never quite seems to work like that. More often than not, our kids see our old toys as vintage junk. Our nostalgia for our toys isn't false or misplaced, but the depth of our feelings was probably enhanced, not only by the years we played with them but also by seeing them advertised on TV. Powerful advertising men like Ray Mithun laid the groundwork for today's complex marketplace of children's digital technology. The world is a vastly different place today from when we were children, but in the business of advertising, the rules are the same. The rules are just being applied in more sophisticated ways through very sophisticated delivery systems.

CHAPTER THREE

THE BROTHERHOOD OF RADIO STATIONS

I got my first job as a radio announcer by lying. I was thirty years old, doing telephone sales jobs, bothering people at all hours of the day and night selling everything from magazine subscriptions to ads in the International Longshoremen & Warehousemen's Union testimonial dinner book. While scanning the *San Francisco Chronicle* help wanted section, I noticed a phone sales job for a local radio station, K-Kiss 99, in suburban Walnut Creek, California. I called, scheduled an interview, and took the BART train for a comfortable twenty-minute ride east into Contra Costa County where well-coifed K-Kiss News Director, Herb Kanner, met me at the train and drove me to the radio station in a fire-engine red Mercedes 450 SEL. He showed me around the neatly appointed station with its new carpet smell and bamboo-paneled walls. Herb took me into his office, put his feet up on his highly polished Hawaiian koa wood desk, and lit a cigarette.

"We're looking for a motivated sales person to sell low-priced, on-air advertising packages over the telephone to beauty parlors, hardware stores, and gas stations. Now, the senior sales guys here will tell you I'm an idiot, that this is low-hanging fruit, easy pickings, but not that lucrative. I know better. There's money to be made here. If I were an idiot, would I be driving the car I drive?"

I took my resumé out of my shirt pocket and slid it across Herb's desk. He glanced at it and said, "You've got a nice voice. You can have the job if you want it. You'll start at 165 dollars a week."

I would have to take a pay-cut in order to work at K-Kiss 99.

"Jimmy Katz at El Dorado Enterprises pays me a lot more. It's going to be hard to leave that job for the money you're offering." I had never played hard-ball in a job interview before. But I needed the money.

I continued working for Jimmy for a few days, selling indulgences to signatories of the ILWU. Then Herb Kanner called from K-Kiss 99.

"What will it take to help you make up your mind?"

I had wanted to work in radio ever since I was twelve years old when I formed the Brotherhood of Radio Stations in South Minneapolis with my friends Steve Gray, John Waterhouse, and Skipper Hastings. I have a theory that the media appeals to the twelve-year-old in us. Today we watch TV, videos, movies, surf the web, and play computer games the way an uncritical twelve-year-old does. As a sixth-grader, my hero and role model was Steve's older brother, Dick. His ham radio shack—a locked room with plywood walls and no windows—was next to the ping-pong table behind the furnace in his basement. We listened through the walls as Dick sent mysterious messages in Morse code to strangers all across the globe from his "ham shack."

From the name, I expected to find cured meats inside. The word "ham" was originally a disparaging nineteenth-century term referring to "ham-fisted" telegraph key operators who were slow at sending Morse code. Dick's ham shack walls were covered with postcards from fellow ham radio operators, and on his desk sat his prized Heathkit HW-101 amateur radio transceiver, a Morse code semi-automatic telegraph key, and a thick coaxial cable snaking up the wall through the ceiling, connecting to a radio antenna on the roof, which allowed Dick to broadcast to fellow ham radio operators around the world. Silvery beads of melted solder, lengths of bell wire, and receipts from Jim's Radio & TV Repair Shop littered his desk.

One Saturday morning, I sat down to watch *Captain Kangaroo* on TV, a program I found detestably simple-minded. But not much else was on, and I was addicted to watching television whenever I could. Just as I turned on the TV, the phone rang. My older brother, Pete, shouted down the basement stairs, "It's for you, jughead. It's your buddy John Waterhouse."

I picked up the phone. John sounded excited. He was out of breath.

"Steve Gray, Skipper Hastings, and I are at Jim's Radio & TV Repair Shop, and Jim just showed us how to turn a radio into a public address system."

I had no idea what this meant, but it sounded important.

"You remove a radio from its case, attach the wires of a microphone to the prongs on the volume control, and your voice comes out of the radio!"

I was awestruck. This was big news. For a twelve-year-old boy, the ability to be louder than usual with the aid of electronics was earth shaking. I met up with John, Skipper, and Steve. We expropriated an old cathedral-shaped AM radio from the Gray's attic and took it down to Dick's ham shack. We tuned the radio to the local rock 'n' roll station, WDGY. They were playing the Everly Brothers' *Wake Up Little Susie*. We plugged in Dick's soldering gun. A thin stream of smoke rose from its metal tip, which glowed red-hot like a tiny branding iron. Steve opened his brother's desk and took out a small plastic grey and white Shure microphone, reached the soldering gun into the back of the radio, and attached the microphone wires to the prongs of the volume control. WDGY fell silent. One by one we took turns speaking into the mic. With an awe I had never felt before, I listened to our scratchy adolescent voices come booming out of the radio. We were on the air.

We raced to the hardware store and bought our own soldering

guns. Then, each of us found an unused radio at home and performed the operation we had learned from Jim's Radio & TV. We wired our houses for sound, running speaker wire down stairways and clothes chutes, placing speakers strategically throughout the house. I purchased a five-watt Knight-kit AM wireless transmitter capable of broadcasting a distance of two-and-a-half houses. I learned this by means of a transmitter strength-test. I sent John Waterhouse out in the street with an AM transistor radio to his ear and instructed him, "Keep waving your arms as long as you can hear my signal." He walked down the sidewalk, and at the first house he waved. At two houses his wave grew a little weaker. By the time he reached the third house, he stopped waving altogether and shrugged. We forged ahead and created broadcast schedules, selected our favorite records, and flooded our homes with music. We read the news. We served as guests on each other's radio shows. Together, we formed the Brotherhood of Radio Stations and pledged to never stop broadcasting.

Eighteen years later, inside the offices of K-Kiss 99, the idea of sitting at a desk working the phones calling beauty parlors and hardware stores seemed unappealing.

I told K-Kiss Sales Manager Herb Kanner, "If you let me write and record the radio spots I sell, I'll take the job."

Herb walked across the hall to General Manager Dick Schofield's office. They chatted for a moment, the GM squinted at me though the glass doors, nodded his head, and Herb returned to his desk.

"You got it, partner."

I quit my job with El Dorado Enterprises and went to work at K-Kiss 99. Members of the sales staff drove leased foreign sports cars to work and sported Italian three-piece suits. I rode the BART train and wore khakis.

Herb handed me a shoebox full of index cards with names and addresses. "Get these people on the phone, sell the heck out of them, and don't leave any money on the table."

Every morning, the K-Kiss 99 bullpen hummed with activity.

Salesmen made appointments with advertisers, called their stock brokers, and arranged to have their expensive leased vehicles washed and waxed. On the first day at work, I made dozens of phone calls but sold nothing. Day two was more successful. I made my first 85-dollar sale to Chipper's Pet Shoppe near the Walnut Creek BART station.

I said to my first client, "Sir, thanks for advertising on K-Kiss. Now would you like me to copy your Yellow Page ad for your radio commercial?"

"No. My wife wrote that. I want something special for the radio. So, Mr. Salesman, what kind of ad will you make for me?" asked Chipper.

I hadn't written a radio commercial since I ran WCLO when I was twelve, so I made it up as I went along.

"Uh, well, have you ever read John Steinbeck's *Grapes of Wrath*?"

"In high school, yeah, why?"

"I am going to do a custom reading of a passage from the book. You'll hear fifty seconds of me reading Steinbeck's brilliant prose followed by, 'This special reading has been brought to you by Chipper's Pet Shoppe, 1871 Ygnacio Valley Road, Walnut Creek, California.'"

"That's my address. What else?"

"How about, 'For the best pet supplies around?'"

"You got it, champ. Send me a copy of the ad, I'll send you a check."

I was in business. I was selling, producing, and voicing radio commercials. I felt important. I could feel my head growing bigger. Did I need an agent? I mailed my Chipper's Pet Shoppe commercial to a local talent agent who, to my great surprise, took me on as a client. The first audition he sent me on was not for a voiceover job but a still photo shoot for Pacific Gas and Electric Company (PG&E), who wanted a photo of an actor squinting at his electric bill, looking horrified. I could do that. When the ad appeared in the local newspaper, I proudly bought a half-dozen copies. On a blind date with a young woman, I showed her my PG&E ad just as one of my commercials came on the car radio. I turned up the volume, " . . . Brought to you by Chipper's Pet Shoppe. "

"So that's you?" she said.

"Yep, that's me."

"Hmm. So how does it feel being surrounded by yourself?"

I never thought of myself as a showboater, but getting this kind of attention was intoxicating. Perhaps there was a place for me in a world that had always held tremendous allure—advertising and the media, a world that prompted rich memories of sitting with my father at work at *Better Homes & Gardens* as he created advertisements.

Soon after I started at K-Kiss 99, the midday announcer retired. I applied for his job and made an appointment to see General Manager Dick Schofield.

"Have you ever been on the air before?" he asked.

"Oh, yes," I lied, "I was Program Director of WCLO AM-1330 in school. I did everything from choosing the music playlist to creating contest giveaways to writing advertising copy." It was true that I was Program Director of WCLO AM-1330. But I was twelve years old at the time, and WCLO was in my bedroom in South Minneapolis.

"Oh, I know all about it, son. I ran the radio station at my college, too. You just earned yourself a raise. You're a radio announcer now."

I neglected to tell him that by "school," I meant primary school, not college. I couldn't help it. This was my dream job, and I couldn't let the opportunity pass me by. I couldn't let the Brotherhood of Radio Stations down.

I have been fascinated with the media from an early age. Had there been video games and the internet when I was a child, I would have been a devoted user. My involvement with media as a youngster led to a life-long career. My friends and I in the Brotherhood of Radio Stations did more than sit by and watch. We took an active hand in shaping our destinies. But as I matured, I began to take a longer view of the media, what it sold, and how it shaped public opinion and the self-image of its audiences.

CHAPTER FOUR

BETTY CROCKER— MEETING THE MYTH

"Son, I've got a big star for you to meet downstairs. Big star. Put your suit jacket on and come down to the living room."

I straightened my tie and followed my dad down the stairs. I was twelve years old. My father was throwing a party for his colleagues at work. The evening was in full swing. My dad wore a double-breasted, pinstriped suit and a pair of black and tan wingtip shoes. He was an advertising executive for General Mills, but he dressed like Vito Corleone in *The Godfather*. My dad grew up poor in the back room of a cigar store on the south side of Chicago, a tough kid from the neighborhood, the perfect preparation to deal with the monolithic power that controlled him at work—The Betty Crocker brand.

My older brother, Pete, and I worked my father's parties as greeters, coat checks, and servers. The guests were advertising executives, copywriters, commercial artists, and radio and TV announcers who did voiceovers for my dad. When our doorbell rang, we sprang into action. My brother carried the guests' coats up to the closet, and I served the hors d'ouvres. I'm not sure why, but the advertising people acted like cattle. When I held up a platter of bacon-wrapped smokies, hands shot out from all sides. No eye contact, no "thank-you's." They stuffed their mouths and made boring grownup conversation. Eventually, my brother relieved me, and my dad took me into the living room. Sitting in an easy chair was a beautiful blonde woman wearing a sleeveless black cocktail dress and a smile as wide as the Mississippi River.

"Son, meet Betty Crocker."

"Betty Crocker? The lady on the cake mix box?"

"That's right."

I stepped forward, feeling rather awkward, and said, "Hello, very nice to meet you."

Betty Crocker offered me her slim, elegant hand. Her skin was smooth and silky.

"Awfully nice to meet you, young man. You're doing a wonderful job at your father's party."

Her voice could have melted glaciers. She smelled of lilacs. Betty Crocker was real.

"Your first big star, right, son? We send her all over the country dressed up like Betty Crocker. She plays Betty Crocker on TV."

"She plays Betty Crocker? Like I play cops and robbers?"

She laughed, and my dad explained, "Son, she's an actress. Her name is Jane Webb. She appears in the Betty Crocker TV ads and narrates the radio commercials. There is no real Betty Crocker."

I was stunned. This icon of American domesticity appeared very real to me. I had seen her on cake mix boxes, in magazines, and on TV. But the Betty Crocker who appeared in print was actually a photographic composite of over a hundred faces of American women. Art directors picked Jane Webb because she looked like the composite photograph. Betty Crocker was a creature of General Mills' corporate imagination. She had been created to sell cake mix.

Decades after I met Betty Crocker, I was hired to be the announcer for a Bank of America radio commercial. The recording engineer for the session escorted me into the large sound-proofed room, adjusted the microphones, and handed out radio scripts. My voiceover partner was an older blonde woman in a matching cranberry skirt, blouse, and jacket. She had a pleasant announcer's voice. She looked vaguely familiar. I told her my name. A look came over her face like she was trying to remember something from a long time ago.

She asked, "Are you by any chance related to Joe Ratner?"

"He was my father."

She threw her arms around me.

"I worked for your dad. I loved your dad. He was the nicest man. He came to work during a recession when General Mills made us all wear buttons that said, 'Save.' Your dad got us buttons that said, 'Spend.'"

It was Jane Webb, the actress who played Betty Crocker in the 1950s.

"You're Betty Crocker. My dad called you 'a big star.'"

I was thrilled to reconnect with Jane. It filled me with memories of my father. Jane squeezed my hand. "And you and I get to work together today."

"It won't be the first time," I said. "The night I met you, I was working at my dad's party. And you were working . . . as Betty Crocker."

"Yes, I was. Being Betty Crocker kept me very busy. She was the second-most popular woman in America back then—second only to Eleanor Roosevelt. Except Eleanor Roosevelt was real. I'm just a voice now. I'm too old to be Betty Crocker. They can never let Betty Crocker age."

It was twenty-five years later, but Jane's voice hadn't aged at all. It was like her voice remembered being Betty Crocker. The human voice is a powerful tool that advertisers and programmers use to get consumers' attention. Until the 1950s, the main source of electronic entertainment for Americans was the radio. Mutual Radio Network, The Radio Corporation of America, NBC Radio, and CBS Radio aired scripted comedies, dramas, news, and variety shows day and night. Families gathered around their cathedral-shaped radios in their living rooms and listened to *The Shadow*, *Lights Out*, *Our Miss Brooks*, *Superman*, *The Orson Welles Radio Hour*, *Harbor Detective*, and many more. Listeners developed deep loyalties for their favorite characters and programs.

When I was fourteen, I spent my spring vacation with my Aunt Eunice and Uncle Gerry in their twenty-ninth-floor penthouse apartment on Lake Shore Drive in Chicago. They knew I was interested in radio, so they took me to the nearby Allerton Tip Top Tap Hotel on Michigan Avenue to see a live broadcast of the Don MacNeill Breakfast Club, which aired five mornings a week on NBC radio. The Breakfast Club ran from 1933 to 1968—thirty-five and a half years—longer than any network radio or TV program in broadcast history. Because of his mellifluous, silky voice and persuasive manner Don MacNeill was a favorite of advertisers who paid top dollar to have him voice their commercials for everything from cigarettes, to roaster ovens, automobiles, and washing machines.

MacNeill was a rather large, pear-shaped, middle-aged man with a rich baritone voice, a pronounced double-chin and a thick mane of brown hair held in place with Vitalis Hair Tonic, and he was the perfect master of ceremonies. For that hour inside the Grand Ballroom of the Allerton Tip Top Tap Hotel I sat back and listened to him purr into his silver RCA ribbon microphone. I was hypnotized. There was magic in his technique. Like all great vocal presenters Don Mac-Neill had perfect control over his voice. He modulated the highs and lows, swooping like an elegant hawk from one sales point to the next, intimate and insinuating, then grand and magnificent.

As I watched Don MacNeill croon his way through his sixty-second radio commercials, I remembered my father's fascination with the early "snake oil salesmen" who roamed American highways and byways from the earliest days of our country, going from town to town in horse-drawn wagons selling potions, tonics, brews, and creams that were alleged to cure whatever ailed you. (Snake oil was the most exotic and purportedly the most powerful of products, descending from the mythic denizens of the Garden of Eden, and modern man had been wily enough to capture and bottle it up for sale to the general public.) My father was born early in the twentieth century on the south side of Chicago where travelling salesmen set up camp in nearby fields and vacant lots. To my dad, they were the best show in town with their wild claims and elastic voices that sang the praises of their products with magical properties. Today, when I watch infomercials on late-night TV for products that promise to give you perfect abs and beautiful buttocks, I have to wonder if advertising has really changed much since the days of the wandering snake oil salesmen.

In the same way that I was hypnotized by radio announcer Don MacNeill when I was fourteen, kids today are lured by well-trained pitchmen on highly sophisticated digital delivery systems. And I happen to be one of those well-trained pitchmen.

I began studying voiceovers from a Chicago radio personality named Joanie Gerber, known for her humorous radio series, "The Chicken Lady." Joanie had flaming red hair, a warm, effusive personality, and the ability to perform dozens of distinctly different voices, each one sounding as real as your next door neighbor. She taught her voiceover workshop at Sound Services, Inc., a popular Hollywood recording studio across from Samuel Goldwyn Movie Studios on Santa Monica Boulevard.

One night in class Joanie sent me into the recording booth, and on the music stand was a voiceover for a popular brand of cat food.

"We are recording, you can go any time," said the audio engineer. I read the spot aloud.

"Bill!" shouted Joanie through the talk-back speaker. "You sound like a phony. I love you, but you don't sound real."

Joanie didn't mince words. And I knew she was right. I was reading the announcer role, and the announcer's job in this particular spot was to convince the audience that if they didn't buy this specific brand of cat food, their pet might not live a full and happy life.

"Joanie, there's something distasteful about this: 'If you don't buy our cat food, your cat may die an untimely death.'"

"Right," said Joanie. "Do you have a problem with that?"

"Yeah, it seems cruel to the audience."

"Look," she said as she got up from her director's chair and stepped inside the recording booth with me. "The character you're playing is the spokesman. He's not you. It's a role you must play as a voice actor if you want to win this job. Just take the money, and feel guilty all the way to the bank."

For Joanie, this wasn't an ethical question. The purpose of a commercial is to sell products. If I wanted to work in voiceovers, I would have to approach each script as an actor would. The "spokesman" in this cat food spot was simply a role. The job of the commercial spokesman is to manipulate the viewer into buying the product. Is this ethical? In the world of commercials, that's a moot point. The point is to sell. There are laws against lying in a commercial, and manufacturers generally don't put sawdust in cat food cans. But there are no laws that can regulate the way advertisers play on our emotions in order to sell you something.

When you wonder why your child spends an inordinate amount of time watching TV, playing video games, or scrolling through YouTube videos, remember that they've been lured to their screens by masters of their craft, highly paid communication experts whose sole responsibility is to secure kids' eyeballs and keep them watching day and night.

PBS journalist Douglas Rushkoff reports that young people are spending upwards of fifty hours a week on digital media, which is supported by advertising revenues.[18] It's impossible to view videos on YouTube without seeing TV commercials repurposed for the web. For parents of young children, in this vast digital marketplace, it's a case of *caveat emptor*—buyer beware.

Advertisers want consumers to stay loyal. The bite out of the apple on Apple Computer products and the friendly face of Betty Crocker on a box of cake mix are images. Advertisers use images to keep us buying. Meeting the actress who played Betty Crocker was an act of unmasking and demystifying an advertising icon. But the image and the idea of Betty Crocker embodied in a simple photo collage and an actress reciting her lines in commercials, created hundreds of millions of dollars of profit for Betty Crocker's creators.

CHAPTER FIVE

MY DAD'S BIG SPEECH

On the way to a Minnesota Gophers football game, my dad pulled into the Nicollet Hotel parking structure.

"Dad, what about the football game?"

"We'll get there, son. I just have to give this little speech."

In addition to his job as an advertising executive, my father was also a paid professional speaker. I had seen him on local TV talk shows introducing famous commercial characters he was responsible for putting on TV—The Pillsbury Doughboy, Betty Crocker, The Hamms Beer Bear. He spoke about advertising with a sense of humor and just a touch of cynicism that always endeared him to his audiences.

We raced into the elevator and rode up to the Grand Ballroom of the hotel where hundreds of businessmen in suits were seated at lunch tables. A man was finishing his prepared speech before the crowd, and just as my father seated me in the front row, the MC announced, "And now, we've got a real treat for you. The Minnesota Marketing Association is proud to introduce the man who will explain it all to you—from marketing to merchandising to the reason we put icing on a cake. Ladies and gentlemen, Mr. Joe Ratner."

Unlike the rest of the men in the ballroom, who were dressed in conservative business suits, my dad wore red slacks and a scotch plaid sports coat with no tie. He was an impressive-looking man, an athlete, with a wide chest and big arms. While other panelists held typed speeches in their hands, my dad took a wrinkled envelope with notes on it from his breast pocket, carefully placed it on the lectern, and proceeded to deliver an amusing and informative speech about the state of advertising. As I sat proudly looking up at him from the front row, he included me in his presentation.

"Now, here's my thirteen-year-old son, Billy. You like hot dogs, don't you, son?"

I stammered, "Yes."

"What do you like on them?"

"Uh, mustard . . . relish . . . ketchup."

"See, my son is a regular consumer . . . of condiments." The audience laughed.

My dad was spontaneous, and enthusiastic in the way he talked about his career. He had come into the "advertising game," as he called it, during the biggest economic boom America has ever known. After World War II, the Great Depression ended, soldiers returned to the home front, and the post-war baby boom followed. Factories hummed, Americans bought new homes and everything to go with them—television sets, washers, dryers, and automobiles. Magazines featured bright new four-color display advertising, and the advertising business was the place to be for an educated, enterprising person. My father went from promoting clean bathrooms at Deep Rock Gas Stations to editing *Better Homes and Gardens* magazine ("B, H, and Goo," as he called it) to engineering the rise of the Betty Crocker cake mix empire at General Mills.

In TV ads, he replaced the old-fashioned baritone-voiced announcers with actors. He injected humor into his ad campaigns. He knew that, during a commercial, audiences had to be engaged right away, or they would tune out. The 1950s was a time of vast reshuffling on the corporate landscape. With consolidation and buyouts, companies were growing larger, and their vast lines of products had to be advertised in order to be sold. Procter & Gamble went from selling only hand soap to selling an array of cleaning products of every kind imaginable. Billboards began to crowd America's roadways. And, as the sheer quantity of commercials grew, advertisers made them more artful and effective, and families stuck by their TV sets and watched more advertising than ever before.

During the Christmas season my dad and I went shopping at Southdale Shopping Center in South Minneapolis. Normally jolly and relaxed, my dad suddenly put his hand on my shoulder and pointed across the wide expanse of marble floor in front of Dayton's Department Store.

"You know that guy?" he asked, pointing to a middle-aged man who stood across the mall looking into a store window.

"I've seen him at parties at our house," I said

"That guy does exactly what I do. He has the same title, the same responsibilities. You know what I do at work, right?"

I had been going to work with my dad on weekends for years. He was an advertising executive. He had a big office, he took meetings, made phone calls, shuffled drawings and photographs around on his desk, and made more phone calls while I played with colored pencils from the Art Department.

He gripped my shoulder and pointed at the man.

"That guy is a thief. An idea thief. He steals other people's ideas and claims that they are his. You'll meet people like that in your life. Watch out."

I had never seen my father so serious, so alarmed and accusatory. He explained that at work they regularly held "brainstorming" sessions at which ad execs, writers, and artists tossed around ideas which they would later present to clients (a process familiar to any loyal *Mad Men* viewer). My father claimed that this man and men like him would listen to ideas in the room and later claim them as their own. I knew there was a lesson here somewhere, otherwise why would my dad have told me about the idea thief? Then he broke into his usual jaunty stride, and we shopped for a Christmas gift for my mom.

I wondered for days what was so important about the ideas this man had allegedly stolen from my father. Was the combined intelligence of top advertising executives valuable enough for someone inside the walls to engage in idea thievery? These were powerful, well-paid executives who were putting ideas into action—a process that involved skill, intelligence, and detailed planning, all focused on one outcome: the sale of a product to the consumer. And the odds appeared to be stacked against the consumer.

Soon after that, my father came home from work one afternoon while my brother and I were doing homework in the living room. He picked up the new edition of *Time* magazine, and said, "This looks like my boss."

He hurled the magazine to the floor and stomped on it. My brother and I thought this was very funny. My dad loved to make us laugh. With his hat and coat on and his briefcase still in his hand, he sat down on the couch.

"Boys, no matter how successful I've gotten, I still have a boss. Don't do what I've done. Hang out your own shingle."

"What does that mean?" I asked

"It means start your own business. Don't go to work for other people. In the old country, where your grandmother comes from, the candlemaker or the tailor rented a storefront and hung up a shingle with his name on it and painted a symbol on it that showed what he did for a living. But sometimes bad men came along and rousted him out for being of a different religion. So the candlemaker would take down his shingle, pack up, move on to the next town, and hang up his shingle again."

My father had always worked for someone else. He hadn't followed his own advice. There was a touch of resentment in the way he told me and my brother this story. I had never noticed that tone from him before.

I heard his cynicism again later that year. He was fifty-one years old. It was icy on the road as my dad drove toward my middle school. He slowed down and honked the horn. Herb, the young ad exec who drove carpool with us, climbed into the front seat. He kept his hat and gloves on. It was a cold Minnesota winter morning. Herb opened his briefcase and pulled out some papers.

"We got the proofs back for the cookbook, Joe. They look good."

As Director of Marketing for the Flour and Mix Division of General Mills, my dad supervised publication of the Betty Crocker cookbook—an annual company tradition and a powerful marketing tool that was advertised on television, featured in bookstores, and ended up under the Christmas trees of millions of American homemakers.

My dad glanced at the bunch of papers and waved them aside.

"The cookie-bookie?" he asked in a mock-foreign accent. My friend Steve and I giggled in the back of the car.

"The what?" asked the junior executive.

"Cookie-bookie?" continued my dad, comically hunched over the steering wheel like a peasant driving a donkey cart.

The young ad exec looked puzzled. My dad wasn't taking him seriously. He had no interest in a serious discussion about the Betty Crocker cookbook. He continued repeating, "Cookie-bookie," and Steve and I continued to laugh. After his final "cookie-bookie," my dad drove the rest of the way to school in silence.

As funny as this seemed to me at the moment, for the first time, I wondered what the future held for him. That year, my dad would get the Betty Crocker cookbook out on time with all its attendant hoopla. But underneath the pride and good cheer, my father was no longer in love with the world of advertising. It had lost its luster. He was at the pinnacle of his long career as a corporate marketing executive, but he mentioned that he wanted to resume his teaching career. He had dedicated thirty years of his life to advertising. Teaching would bring in only a fraction of the salary he earned as an executive, but that didn't seem to matter.

Sadly, not long after his animated display in carpool, poking fun at the centerpiece of his marketing career, my father died of a sudden heart attack.

Career-wise, I took my father's advice. Aside from a few years working for a corporate-owned radio station, I have carved out a career as a freelance voiceover announcer. I'm not stuck in an office nine-to-five. My dad would be happy to know that I am my own boss. But I do work in essentially the same business as he did—the "advertising game." If my father were alive today and could see all the gadgets that surround me and his grandchildren, he would be amused, fascinated, and a bit cynical about it all, I'm sure.

What I learned from my father is what allowed me to write this book. Watching TV with my dad was an education in itself. As the programs and commercials played, he offered critiques, analyses, and funny voices. I think of my dad often, especially when I have a chance to pass on to others what he taught me. I learned that the combined intelligence of tens of thousands of highly educated advertising experts are focused on one target—you, the consumer. My father saw through the smoke and mirrors of the commercial world, and so must we.

CHAPTER SIX

BARBIE

I sat on the floor playing Barbies with my six-year-old daughter, Arianna. It was 1993. To my relief, she wasn't terribly interested in Barbie's vast fashion collections, but she was definitely into making up dialogue.

"Okay," she said, pulling her half-clad Barbies out of a cardboard shoebox and arranging them on the floor. "I don't have a Ken doll, which is fine," she said, "because he's kind of a dork, so you are going to be, I don't know . . . somebody."

"I've got a G.I. Joe in the other room if you think he'd play well with Barbie," I said.

"No, dad, G.I. Joe is gross. We're not playing war, we're playing Barbies."

When playing Barbies, my daughter was in charge. To make her authority perfectly clear, Arianna had removed Barbie's clothes and kept them neatly arranged in plastic containers that she opened for friends.

Barbie served the same purpose for my daughter that dolls have served for children since prehistoric times: they are malleable characters that speak dialogue created by children in the drama of life. Children have always played with toy human figures. Contemporary archeologists report that figurines unearthed at antiquity sites, once thought to be idols of ancient deities, are usually dolls and toys used by children in much the same way as modern toys are used: to engage the users in the traditional activity of children—make believe.

German cultural historian Max Von Boehn writes in his book, *Dolls*, "If the genesis of the doll is sought for, it will be found . . . in a quality which is shared alike by primitive races and by children—namely the ability to discern human and animal forms."[19]

Children have always picked up a stick, an ear of corn, a crudely whittled figure, and "seen" a human face, imagined its human characteristics, and brought the object to life by imagining words and actions. But with carefully crafted modern toys, children's imaginative play can be limited by the nature of the toy itself and by the profit motive of the toymaker. Hasbro's G.I. Joe encourages the purchase of an ever-expanding team of military action figures and accessories. Mattel's Barbie encourages serial doll outfit consumption.

My daughters are among the vast majority of girls who own Barbies. Mattel claims that 90 percent of American girls, age three to eleven, own at least one Barbie doll. Over a billion Barbies have been sold since she started rolling off her Japanese assembly line in 1959. Reportedly, every two seconds, somewhere in the world a new Barbie doll is purchased—40 percent outside the United States. The Barbie brand is worth over two billion dollars, putting it ahead of Armani, just behind Dow Jones Corporation—making it the most valuable toy brand in the world.

In the pre-Barbie era, doll manufacturers catered to the belief that baby dolls encouraged the mothering instinct in little girls. But Barbie was designed for a new purpose. Her creator, Mrs. Ruth Handler, co-founder of Mattel, watched her young daughter Barbara play with paper dolls rather than traditional baby dolls. She preferred paper dolls because she and her friends could dress them up in interchangeable outfits and create fashions with paper and scissors. Paper dolls were more grown up than baby dolls. But paper dolls couldn't stand, sit, or gesture very well.

In the 1950s the US toy market was dominated by competing brands of baby dolls. Miss Revlon High Heeled Fashion Doll wore attractive dresses, but like most of her doll competitors, she had chubby little arms and legs and round, puffy cheeks, just like a baby. The popular Ideal Boopsie Doll had a hard plastic jointed body, molded painted hair, and came dressed in a cotton diaper closed with a safety pin. Doll manufacturers catered to what they thought were mothers' wishes—that little girls should use dolls and doll-play to prepare for life as a parent. Ideal Toy Company's Betsy Wetsy's accessories included baby bottles, layettes, a bathtub, and baby clothing. And for those industrious mothers and daughters who wanted to make baby clothes for Betsy Wetsy, she also came with baby clothing patterns. And for those who wanted their dolls to perform bodily functions, requiring cleanup and diapering—or, as the package advertised, "Doing What Comes Naturally"—there was the Little Squirt doll.

But Barbie was not a baby doll. At first, her mature teen appearance was a stumbling block for Mattel. The company's first big financial success was co-founder Elliot Handler's creation, the Thunderburp Tommy Gun, which fired explosive caps like the traditional toy cap pistol, only much faster, like a fully-automatic machine gun, going through a roll of caps in a matter of seconds. Mattel took smart advantage of opportunities in the post–World War II toy marketplace. Toy advertising on television in the 1950s was virtually non-existent except during the pre-Christmas shopping season. At the time of Barbie's creation, toys were advertised mainly in store catalogues, with ads directed at parents, not children. Mattel's first TV commercial for the Thunderburp Tommy Gun aired in the premier episode of Walt Disney's TV show *The Mickey Mouse Club*. Mattel soon became the chief sponsor of Disney's hit television franchise. The commercial featured a close-up follow shot of a little boy carrying his Thunderburp

Tommy Gun through his living room while imagining "hunting elephants in Africa." At the end of the commercial, the announcer said, "Don't worry. The Burp Gun is so safe, it's got the Parents Seal of Approval." But critics felt that the unveiling of the surprisingly realistic-looking Thunderburp Tommy Gun marked the beginning of a new era in toys when children's play became focused on the toy itself as an object of wonder, rather than a simple vehicle for make-believe. When Barbie and her many outfits rolled off the assembly line, she was accused of the same thing—encouraging consumerism in children rather than imaginative doll-play.

Mattel co-founder Ruth Handler was travelling with her children in Europe in 1956 when she spotted a sexy, grownup-looking, twelve-inch doll in a tobacco store window in Frankfurt, Germany. The doll's name, she learned, was Bild Lilli, based on a character in a comic strip that ran in the popular German tabloid magazine, Bild Zeitung. Bild Lilli was produced as a promotional item for the magazine's advertisers. The doll proved popular, and demand for her grew. Bild Lilli was referred to as a "sex toy," and she was sold mainly to men in tobacco stores and bars. Women bought the doll for their husbands as a joke gift. The doll was dressed as her namesake character in the comic strip—a sassy, fashionable, independent, 1950s working girl who was unafraid to state her opinion of things. The doll wore eye makeup, short skirts, and stylish outfits, and had realistic-looking hair that could be brushed and styled. She came with interchangeable outfits and accessories. And for the first time in the history of commercial doll making, Bild Lilli had a well-developed bust line.

For Ruth Handler, discovering Bild Lilli in that German tobacco store window was a life-changing event. Bild Lilli embodied nearly everything Ruth's daughter Barbara and her friends wanted in a doll—a toy that little girls could dress up, that would be the child's equal, a fashionable companion. Bild Lilli was a very grownup doll that looked "real." Handler purchased three Bild Lilli dolls from the German tobacconist, gave one to her daughter Barbara and brought the other two back to the designers at Mattel. Handler moved fast and secured the rights to manufacture the doll in Japan and market her in the United States. She renamed the doll "Barbie," after her daughter, Barbara.

Ruth Handler demanded of her designers that Barbie look "real." Though Barbie was virtually identical to Bild Lilli, she would be called "Barbie, the Teenage Fashion Model"—a young career girl who wore a black and white zebra-striped swimsuit, high heels, a stylish ponytail (available in blond or brunette). Barbie came with accessories, numerous outfits, and made-up eyes coquettishly averted to the side. After designers found the right soft vinyl material from which Barbie could be manufactured, furious debates erupted within Mattel's Hawthorne, California, headquarters over whether or not Barbie should have breasts as prominent as Bild Lilli's.

Ruth's husband, Elliot, felt the bosomy prototypes were too provocative for the toy market. But Ruth moved ahead with production, employing clothing designers and seamstresses to create thirty interchangeable outfits for Barbie. Her debut took place at Toy Fair 1956 in New York. Reception was mixed. Most of the professional toy store buyers at the time were men. They expressed surprise and shock at Barbie's mature teen hips, long legs, and bust line, and asked, "What mother is going to buy a toy for her young daughter that looks like that?" Large retail stores stayed away from Barbie. It was a difficult first year.

Undaunted, Ruth Handler forged ahead. She hired a Viennese psychoanalyst—a refugee from World War II named Ernst Dichter. As a trained psychotherapist, Dichter knew his way around both the human mind and the advertising world, having consulted for marketing departments of major US advertisers. He founded his consulting practice on the belief that humans are impressionable, emotional, and irrational.[20] We buy things we don't need, often at arbitrary prices, and for silly reasons. Over one hundred years ago, Sigmund Freud argued that people are governed by irrational, unconscious urges.

Dichter spun this belief into a million-dollar consulting business. For Mattel, Dichter interviewed dozens of little girls and their mothers, asking about their objections to the new Barbie doll. The mothers expressed shock at Barbie's grown up appearance. But their daughters disagreed. They felt that Barbie, with her numerous outfits and fashion accessories, offered far more creative play opportunities than any doll they'd ever seen. They liked changing her clothes, styling her hair, and helping Barbie get ready for the world. Through the use of focus groups, Dichter found the greatest obstacle to selling Barbie was the resistance of the mothers. So he set about influencing the way Barbie was portrayed in commercials, convincing mothers that Barbie, through her extensive wardrobe, would teach little girls how to present themselves to the world in a polished way. Barbie's earliest TV commercials featured pre-teen actresses play-acting as customers in a grownup-looking boutique with a store clerk who showed samples of Barbie's vast wardrobe, "Everything from a basic wardrobe to the most gorgeous designer creations," says the clerk in the commercial. "Which ones would you like?"

"I think we'd like all of them," say the little girls. ("All of them" would have cost them far more than their childhood allowance would ever have allowed.)

Barbie's TV ads told kids that when the seasons change, so does fashion, and to keep up with the Joneses, you must buy Barbie a new wardrobe. Mattel's TV ads encouraged serial consumerism, with the major focus of play being the dressing of Barbie.

Barbie has changed with the times. The 1960s saw her wearing more casual outfits. The '70s brought us Disco Barbie. In the '80s, celebrity artist Andy Warhol painted pictures of Barbie, while the '90s brought us Desert Storm Barbie. The world's greatest fashion designers—Christian Dior, Bill Blass, Oscar de la Renta, Vera Wang, Carolina Herrera—have all designed clothes for Barbie. Plus, Barbie is quite comfortable in today's wired world with an extensive internet presence. To date, Barbie has had more than 120 careers— from an Olympic gold medalist to a US Air Force pilot—and she has rep-resented fifty different nationalities. Mattel claims many personal victories amongst fans due to Barbie's "positive influence," such as the young girl who wanted to be a school teacher after her mother bought her "School Teacher Barbie;" the young woman is now a lit-erature professor at a prestigious university, says Mattel. Mattel touts the story of a Barbie fan having Barbie present at the birth of all of the girl's actual pets. Now the young woman runs a local Humane Society. Mattel claims that Barbie taught these girls that they could be anything they wanted to be.

However, Barbie detractors claim that with her impossibly long legs, unrealistically narrow waist, and prominent bust line, Barbie is a destructive force on the self-image of women. Barbie and her in-herent physical limitations—arms that don't bend, a body that can't stand on its own, legs out of proportion to its torso—seem to have much in common with primitive cave drawings—a limited view of human anatomy. Critics claim that little girls grow up believing they are not pretty enough or loveable enough because they don't look like Barbie.

Author Tanya Lee Stone in her book *The Good, The Bad, and The Barbie*, writes of, "A story of brilliant and relentless marketing to children."[21] Polarization of opinion and deep emotion have swirled around Barbie since she first rolled off Mattel's assembly line. Stone floated media queries for opinions about Barbie via the internet, which resulted in hundreds of email responses—half of them neg-ative and half positive. Some women reminisced wistfully and some angrily about their relationships with Barbie. The wide range of opinion about Barbie's worth as a positive fantasy enabler and as a self-image destroyer, mixed with the opinions of journalists and writers, presents a nuanced, complex portrait of three generations of toy consumers and a stupendous marketing success by Mattel.

Amidst the angry anti-Barbie arguments and pro-Barbie senti-ments, one of the most sanguine and realistic opinions comes from

British journalist Ann Treneman, who wrote in *The Independent* in 1999, "Little girls take something that is unreal, like Barbie, and make her real through both play and neglect. Barbie herself may be passive, but the world that little girls create is not. Perhaps it is time the grownups started being sensible about it all. All we are talking about here is a bit of curved plastic who has managed to achieve icon status by decades of clever marketing."

In 1993, a clandestine group of artists in New York formed the Barbie Liberation Organization (BLO), dedicated to exposing what they felt were sexual stereotypes being purveyed by Mattel's Barbie dolls and Hasbro's G.I. Joe action figures. BLO operatives purchased 150 new Teen-Talk Barbies and 150 G.I. Joe Talking Duke dolls. They brought the dolls back to their headquarters, stripped the dolls of their dresses and military gear, swapped their electronic voice chips, and created a mutant army of surgically altered dolls. They carefully placed the doctored dolls back into their original packaging and snuck the dolls back onto the shelves in toy stores all across the country.

Christmas morning 1993, children ran to the Christmas tree to see what Santa brought them. "Look, son, it's a brand new G.I. Joe Talking Duke doll. Open him up, and press the bullet on his bandolier and see what he says."

And out of G.I. Joe's mouth came a girlish giggle, "I'm not very good at math. Do you girls want to go shopping with me at the mall?"

Meanwhile, across town: "Look, Mommy, Santa brought me a brand new Teen-Talk Barbie."

"Oh, that's wonderful, honey. Press the pretty green emerald on her necklace and see what Barbie has to say."

And Barbie said in a husky, masculine voice, "Attack! Attack!! Dead men tell no tales. Revenge is sweet. Die, Cobra, die!"

In addition to swapping the voice chips on three hundred dolls, inside the packaging of each of the altered dolls, the BLO had placed a manifesto asking consumers to contact their local media outlets if they agreed that these dolls perpetuated damaging sexual stereotypes. The BLO issued a videotaped statement to the press, featuring a Barbie doll on-camera who said, "I'm Teen-Talk Barbie, the spokesdoll for the BLO. We're an international group of children's toys who are rebelling against the companies that made us. We've turned against our creators because they use us to brainwash children. They build us in a way that perpetuates gender-based stereotypes that have a negative effect on children's development. In order to correct this problem we have set up our own hospitals where we are carrying out corrective surgery on ourselves."

National and local media covered the event extensively. Children and parents were interviewed. Kids found it comical. Grownups' reactions ranged from wan smiles to angry sneers. Neither Mattel nor Hasbro were amused. People came down on both sides of the sexual stereotype argument in equal numbers. In addition to the Barbie Liberation Organization, many artists have had their way with Barbie to the amusement of some and the distaste of others. Some artists who use Barbie as their medium are shown on the website alteredbarbie. com featuring such creations as Biker Crone Barbie, Black Widow Barbie, Saint Barbara, and Not Your Daughter's Barbie.

In 1994, Barbie celebrated her thirty-fifth birthday. After dozens of careers, videos, novels, TV shows, vehicles, homes, and clothing lines, Mattel felt it was time for Barbie to have a signature voice. They put out an audition call to Hollywood voiceover agents to submit their best prospective Barbie voices. Thirty-five-year-old Chris Anthony-Lansdowne was already performing voices for assorted toy lines. Chris's audition was scheduled for the day the Northridge, California, earthquake struck. Chris lived in Northridge, and the water and power were out, freeways were gridlocked, but the telephone lines were working. Chris auditioned as Barbie on the phone. Mattel liked what they heard. They scheduled a call-back for the next day. With water and power still out, Chris tied her hair into a ponytail, put on a baseball cap, and drove south on the 405 Freeway to Mattel

Headquarters in El Segundo, California. She was escorted past the larger-than-life Barbie statue, which dominated the lobby, and was taken to the recording booth. A half-dozen Mattel executives sat on the other side of the sound-proof glass.

Chris glanced at the script and leaned into the microphone, "Hi, it's me, Barbie. You look cool!"

Mattel staffers stared at each other. The director pressed the talk-back button in the control room, "Chris, could you start tomorrow morning? We'd like you to be Barbie for a while."

Chris was thrilled. She remembered back to when she argued with her sister for the right to be Barbie's voice when they played dolls in their bedroom together. The next morning, Chris reported for work. Her first project was Super Talk Barbie. No more putting your finger in a ring to pull a string to make the doll talk; a new sophisticated electronic voice chip was being put into Barbie. She was being programmed to say over a hundred phrases. Super-talk Barbie had been around for a few years, and her voice was rather mature-sounding. Chris's Barbie voice was different. It was girlish, earnest, and enthusiastic. For the next eight years, Chris recorded hundreds of voice tracks for Barbie dolls, games, TV shows, and commercials.

Today, Barbies continue to fill store shelves across the globe. Barbie's recent credits include a new live stage musical touring internationally, a new web series, and a major live-action motion picture. Barbie is still contributing to Mattel's bottom line, and little girls on every continent on earth continue to play with Barbie.

We have always been able to count on the ingenuity and imagination of children to shape doll play to their own particular ends. But when you visit the new, highly controlled Barbie environments at shop.mattel.com, "Styled by Me" webpages take children into a virtual online world, where they "dress" an array of Barbies in virtual outfits and accessories. While the child is on the computer, there is no longer a doll in her hand. Other than the narrow avenues of choice offered by the Barbie website designers, there appears to be little room for imagination. The addictive quality of computer environments for children is a powerful lure. This makes old-fashioned Barbie doll play seem quaint and far more creative than switching virtual outfits by tapping a keyboard in cyberspace.

CHAPTER SEVEN

TV CARTOON BONANZA: THE *G.I. JOE* CHRONICLES

I got my first taste of *G.I. Joe* fandom in New York City's St. Mark's Comics store. Out of curiosity, I stepped into the venerable comic book store and perused the crowded shelves. The last episodes of the animated *G.I. Joe* TV show had been produced over twenty-five years earlier, so I figured the chances were slim that I would find any vintage G.I. Joe action figures. But I asked the young clerk, "You have any *G.I. Joe* stuff?"

He gave me a look that said, *Why is this middle-aged guy lurking around my comic book store?*

"I don't know, maybe over there," he said dismissively, pointing to the crowded action figure rack.

I responded in my no-nonsense, G.I. Joe Flint voice, "Yeah, I get it, kid. And knowing is half the battle. Flint says, 'Yo, Joe.'"

The clerk stared at me for a moment and then walked quickly to the back of the store. A few minutes later, he reappeared carrying a mint-condition comic book in a plastic sleeve, *G.I. Joe: A Real American Hero*, "Side by Side with Destro."

"Flint. I'm sorry, I didn't know who you were, so I Googled you. I'd like to offer you this comic book as a gift, along with a lifetime 10 percent discount on any merchandise in the store."

I had a fan. The young man's attitude had gone from distrust to admiration when he learned that I was the voice of a character on *G.I. Joe*. I mentioned the incident to my wife and daughters. They were amused. I thought about this incident for days. What had affected this young man so deeply? What was his emotional tie to a nearly three-decades-old animated children's television show?

———

On a bright August afternoon in rural New Hampshire in 2008— many years after the premier of the G.I. Joe TV cartoon, I sat on the lawn outside Camp Windsor Mountain's mess hall with a dozen adolescent kids. I was teaching a class in media-related issues. We talked about what teenagers watch on TV, how much time they spend online, whether they watch TV programs on their smartphones, and what they think of commercials.

Zack, a pudgy, curly-haired thirteen-year-old, was a G.I. Joe fan. He boasted an extensive collection of G.I. Joe action figures and DVDs of the TV cartoon.

I asked Zack, "How much money do you think you'd have to spend for one of each of the G.I. Joe action figures and attack vehicles."

Zack rubbed his hands together and excitedly began his calculations. "I figure if you count every member of the G.I. Joe Team—and there are a zillion of them—and if you add in the attack vehicles, you'd have to spend maybe a thousand bucks."

Bebe, a tall, eighth-grade girl from Brooklyn, New York, rolled their eyes. "More," she said. "The Lady Jaye doll alone costs $16.99."

Zack fired back, "That doll is from *G.I. Joe: The Rise of Cobra*, the movie, stupid. We're talking about the original Hasbro TV action figures—Flint, Duke, Scarlett, Lady Jaye—not the movie ones."

Bebe scratched her chin. "By my best calculation, I figure roughly eighteen hundred dollars," she said.

Zack sneered. "That's '80s money. By today's standards with eBay and everything, it's got to be more like five thousand bucks."

This is the kind of conversation that truly excites corporate marketing executives. While our group of young consumers calculated how much it would cost to own the complete collection of G.I. Joe action figures and vehicles, I could almost hear the distant sound of NASDAQ bells ringing up the price of Hasbro common stock.

To wrap up the afternoon, I asked the kids to improvise a skit about the power of television. "Who would like to play The TV Set, and who would like to be The Viewer?" I asked.

Zack jumped to his feet and struck a heroic pose. "Television is not a flesh-and-blood thing," he said dramatically. "It has no jaws filled with sharp teeth, nor muscular, clawed legs. Television is quintessentially a box, a loud and relentless tool operated by a class of corporations so powerful that we are helpless to defend ourselves from its potent, hypnotizing pixels of red, green, and blue that mesmerize us as we watch. Like in *Alice in Wonderland*, the TV propels us to the other side of the magic mirror. And every seven minutes, the on-screen drama comes to a halt as they show us commercials that spring into our brains. Television is there to sell us snacks. We sit by, passive, hungry, in need of stimulation. We belong to the TV, and we are its prey." Zack bowed as enthusiastic applause came from the group.

Bebe took off her glasses and stepped toward Zack. "Back off, monster. We serve you not. You are a ghost ship fouling my horizon. You lurk, sizing me up, along with others who are drawn to you. And as if in a dream, I open myself to you, barren, mindless, and numb. But I am full of hope, because you make me more than I am. You caress my eyes and my heart, and I succumb. I want to be shaped, sheared, and transformed by you into whatever it is you tell me I can be. And I will buy. I will consume. I am undernourished and thirsty, and you are my well of hope. You provide me with a dream of love and relationship."

More applause erupted from the group of adolescents who, when allowed the time to discuss, critique, and air their impressions of electronic media, have strong feelings and opinions. They seem to understand what TV is all about, exhibiting an awareness that will affect their viewing habits and enable them to understand its motives, and appraise it with a critical eye. And at the same time, with all their apparent media smarts, these kids seemed uncritically mesmerized by the characters and toys from a vintage TV cartoon.

In 1982, I was cast as the voice of "Flint," a.k.a. Warrant Officer Dashiell R. Faireborn, in Hasbro's TV cartoon *G.I. Joe: A Real American Hero*. Episodes of *G.I. Joe* aired in syndication and reruns for nearly twenty years in the United States and Britain, and for two years in Hong Kong before Peoples Republic of China broadcast officials figured out that *G.I. Joe* was a profit center and scrapped the English-speaking soundtrack. As Flint mouthed, "Yo, Joe!" in China, Mandarin was heard coming from his heroic lips.

Born from the pen of Hasbro writer/animator Larry Hama, the *G.I. Joe* animated character Flint came with an impressive fictional biography: Flint was a Rhodes Scholar who held a degree in English Literature, graduated with top honors from Airborne School, Ranger School, Special Forces School, and Flight Warrant Officers School, and was a master military tactician. Flint was the soldier I dreamed of being as a kid as I played with my olive drab plastic World War II soldiers. Hasbro recruited Hollywood's best episodic TV and cartoon writers and animators to come up with the characters for the *G.I. Joe* team. And Hasbro took the toy market by storm with action figures of Flint, Lady Jaye, Scarlett, Duke, Cobra Commander, and Destro, to name just a few of the Joes and their Cobra enemies.

Millions of young fans rushed home from school every weekday afternoon to catch a glimpse of their favorite Joes in syndicated episodes of the TV cartoon. Young viewers flocked to comic book stores and toy marts to buy the latest *G.I. Joe* action figures, vehicles, video games, board games, hats, t-shirts, lunch boxes, and kites, resulting in the meteoric rise of the price of Hasbro stock in the early 1980s.

On the first day of voice recording in Wally Burr Recording in Studio City, California, voice actors lined up at the microphones and the *G.I. Joe* script assistant gave us some financial advice.

"I've been told to tell you to buy Hasbro stock," she said as she handed us our scripts.

Someone was trying to do us a favor, but in order to avoid charges of insider trading, they couldn't reveal the fact that, along with the launch of the syndicated TV show *G.I. Joe*, Hasbro had planned a massive rollout of *G.I. Joe* toys and action figures. If each of us had purchased one thousand dollars' worth of shares of Hasbro, Inc., common stock in the autumn of 1982, those shares would have been worth twenty-five thousand dollars in just a few short years. Oh, the heartache of hindsight.

Then the script assistant announced, "No one dies in *G.I. Joe.*"

"No one dies? But it's a war cartoon," said one of the deep-voiced actors.

"Parent groups have gotten involved," she explained, "and they don't want their kids watching a TV cartoon with characters getting shot and dying."

So, when a member of the Joe Team or an enemy from Cobra gets blasted out of the sky, they parachute out over the horizon and show up in a later episode or get written out of the show. Attacking global terrorism with lots of cool weapons and massive fire-fights, and no one dies? How does that happen? I was impressed by the power of parents to sway Hasbro's storylines. But the show still went on.

In the case of *G.I. Joe*, parent media watchdog groups had begun actively following the entertainment news pertaining to children's TV productions. Parents' concerns stemmed from evidence that children imitate violence and stunts they see on television. Social scientists and psychologists don't know the long-term effects on young viewers of watching on-screen violence. There is speculation that playing violent video games and watching violent TV programming can make children more fearful of the world and can desensitize them to violence that occurs in real life.

Parents spoke up, and Hasbro listened. There is a long-standing American tradition of pressure groups staging well-publicized boycotts of products, programs, networks, and corporations, causing media executives' blood to run cold and to make changes that will appease the boycotters. As a result of parent involvement, no one dies in *G.I. Joe*.

The FCC passed The Children's Television Act in 1990, requiring TV stations and networks to monitor their children's programming for violence and other negative programming elements. The act also required television to provide "educational" programs for children. But many parent groups feel the act was ineffective, and that stations and networks actually reduced their commitment to educational programming and simply labeled their commercial programs as "educational."

What led up to production of the *G.I. Joe* TV series and the initial release of *G.I. Joe* toys was one of the most carefully calculated incremental toy merchandising game plans in the history of toy sales. After decades of off-and-on success with brands like Romper Room and Mr. Potato Head, Hasbro struggled in the 1970s with flagging interest in its G.I. Joe brand. The negative association with the Vietnam War, plus the phenomenal success of the Star Wars brand, had weakened sales for Hasbro. Originally, G.I. Joe was a twelve-inch action figure, similar in stature to Mattel's legendary Barbie doll. The full-sized, twelve-inch G.I. Joe was more expensive to produce than the smaller, more lucrative six-inch action figures George Lucas began selling after the 1977 release of the first Star Wars movie.

Hasbro President and CEO Stephen Hassenfeld, third generation head of the family-run corporation, wanted to come up with something to compete with George Lucas's blockbuster Star Wars brand. So Hassenfeld, writer/animator Larry Hama, and Hasbro Product Manager Kirk Bozigian brainstormed. They wanted to make their G.I. Joe action figures cheaper for young consumers than the Star Wars figures. If George Lucas made his action figures six inches tall, Hasbro would make theirs three-and-three-quarters inches tall, cutting manufacturing costs considerably. And they wanted to advertise the new *G.I. Joe* action figures not only in TV commercials, but also within the TV program itself

Standing in their way was the Federal Communications Commission (FCC) and its tough, pro-children TV commercial regulations. (George Lucas wasn't constrained by such rules because his characters were in the movies, not on television.) How could Hasbro get around the FCC's tough rules?

In the early 1980s, national advertisers and the broadcast networks were feeling the effects of an economic recession and were looking for relief. They found a friend in the White House. Before being elected, Governor of California Ronald Reagan's Hollywood acting career had floundered. But he found new employers in the commercial sector—national TV advertisers. He became the on-camera host for the popular TV series *General Electric Theater*, which required him to tour G.E. Plants, give speeches on behalf of the company, and appear in promotional films. Later, he hosted the popular TV series *Death Valley Days*. Reagan was an attractive and skilled on-camera communicator, and he was drafted to run for Governor of the State of California, and, soon, was elected President of the United States.

In 1982, skillful lobbyists, employed by broadcasters and national advertisers, pressured President Reagan, the Federal Communications Commission, and the Federal Trade Commission for greater freedom to advertise inside children's television shows. Washington agreed, and the rules were changed. (Broadcastlawblog.com writes, "In the 1980s, the FCC looked at the competitive marketplace as justification for deregulation.")

For decades, media professionals, educators, and child development experts have felt that children under the age of seven are unable to tell the difference between commercials, fiction programming, and reality on television. That gives advertisers an unfair advantage over young viewers. So, in the 1940s, the FCC drafted regulations to limit TV ads within television programs aimed at children, prohibiting the advertising of action figures inside a show in which the advertised characters appear.

Hasbro learned that it wasn't illegal to run TV ads advertising a *comic book* featuring the action figures in a TV show. Hasbro approached comic book companies with an enticing offer. If they would publish a run of G.I. Joe comics, Hasbro would air well-produced television ads for the comic books inside episodes of *G.I. Joe*. Comic book publishers didn't have the budgets to advertise on television, so when Hasbro executives approached Marvel Comics with their unusual offer, Marvel said, "Yes." And one of the nerviest and boldest children's TV advertising campaigns was born.

Hasbro and Marvel artists went to work expanding the size of the G.I. Joe Team to over a hundred different characters. Writers worked up scripts, animators tooled up for a long run of shows, and the comic book presses rolled into action, cranking out dozens of editions of G.I. Joe comics for Hasbro.

Hasbro master writer/animator Larry Hama designed and wrote the new TV commercials for the Marvel G.I. Joe comic books that would run inside episodes of *G.I. Joe: A Real American Hero*. Both the commercials and the episodes of the TV show were photographed with a level of animation artistry that had never been seen on television before.

Inside each new episode, Hasbro ran their new TV commercials for the G.I. Joe comic books featuring G.I. Joe Team action figures bounding across the screen in a blaze of glory and heroically trouncing the bad guys of Cobra. The G.I. Joe action figures, vehicles, and play sets hit store shelves like an explosion. And G.I. Joe became a toy retailer's dream—a marketing juggernaut so powerful that Hasbro's common stock became a goldmine for stockholders, caused by a few strokes of a pen in Washington, DC, and a brilliant Hasbro marketing strategy.

Hasbro decided to create a quality television program. They enlisted Hollywood animation company Sunbow Productions to handle the physical production of the *G.I. Joe* TV episodes, and they spared no expense. They employed Japanese anime studios in Tokyo to provide technical assistance for animation processes that had not been done on American television before, such as the film techniques of zooming, panning, and tilting. (Walt Disney had mastered film animation techniques that weren't used on TV because of budgetary concerns.) Hasbro wanted its new syndicated TV shows to look more like movies and less like unsophisticated-looking American TV cartoons. (*Clutch Cargo* comes to mind, in which only the character's mouths move while they float stiffly past frozen, stationary backdrops.)

Initially, Hasbro produced a five-episode *G.I. Joe* mini-series that featured a handful of Joe Team and Cobra characters. The response from young viewers was instantaneous. TV ratings were spectacularly successful for the five episodes, and G.I. Joe toy sales skyrocketed. Hasbro followed the mini-series with four years of *G.I. Joe* animated episodes and an animated 1987 feature, *G.I. Joe: The Movie*, starring Don Johnson of *Miami Vice* as the voice of Lt. Falcon. Voice actors collected residual checks through the Screen Actors Guild for nearly twenty years as episodes of *G.I. Joe* ran repeatedly in syndication, reaching two generations of viewers.

To cast the voices of *G.I. Joe*, Hasbro held one of the largest voice acting auditions in the history of Hollywood. I got the call from my agent to show up on a Tuesday morning. On a warm Southern

California day, actors lined up outside Wally Burr Recording on Ventura Boulevard just west of Universal Studios. The line of auditioning voice actors stretched out the door, down the steps, and around the block. On the sidewalk, dozens of actors studied their script pages and rehearsed their lines, barking military orders and grunting and groaning as if in fights to the death with imaginary foes. Hasbro provided the actors with cartoon sketches of the characters. We were auditioning to be heroes—the G.I. Joe Team—and bad guys bent on destroying the world—members of an international terrorist organization known as Cobra.

A low, unearthly growl welled up in the throat of an attractive young woman who stood behind me in line, her brow wrinkled in intense concentration.

"You're toast, Cobra Commander!" Taking a big breath, she shouted to no one in particular, "Yo, Joe!"

"What role are you auditioning for," I asked.

"Lady Jaye," she said breathlessly. "She's a highly trained counter-insurgency operator. My name's Mary. You?"

"Flint . . . I mean Bill. My name is Bill." I glanced at the cartoon sketch on my script. Flint was a handsome, heroic-looking soldier with camouflage gear, a black beret, a nasty-looking automatic rifle, and big pectoral muscles. This was definitely not type-casting, as I was a paunchy thirty-five-year-old radio announcer hoping to land a voice acting role in the new Hasbro TV cartoon.

There is less at stake at a voiceover audition than at an on-camera casting call where an actor's face, hair, and body type are all being scrutinized. Voice actors don't have to look like the characters they are trying out for; they just have to sound like them. Their job is to give the illusion of reality.

I finally made it to the head of the line and was called into the voiceover booth. Wally Burr's studio was roomy and comfortable. Leather couches lined the walls, and there were more microphones set up than I'd ever seen in one studio.

"Take microphone number seven," Wally said into the talkback. He sat behind a large mixing console surrounded by Hasbro and Sunbow executives, writers, and animators whispering directions to Wally who translated them into short, pithy commands for the actors. Wally had a deep, imposing voice, probably something like what Flint should sound like.

"Alright," Wally said, "in this scene Flint is fighting for his life. He's engaged in hand-to-hand combat with a prehistoric dragon who's got him pinned down and is about to sink his fangs into his neck."

I took a last look at the sketch of my well-muscled special ops character.

"Alright, give it a shot. Here is Bill as Flint, take 67A."

I barked out my few short lines of dialogue. It took all of ten seconds. Wally pressed the talkback button.

"Faster, louder, more force from your gut. I'm directing for realism here, pal. You're not going to fool me with dramatics. I was the youngest tank commander in World War II, Captain Wally Burr, so I know this stuff first-hand. Give it all you've got. Take 67B."

I tightened my gut and shouted my words again.

"Good. That's more like it. Third time's the charm. Go all the way with this one. Take 67C."

I closed my eyes, growled, and grunted, and when I finished, I half-expected applause, but I was met with silence. No one was paying attention. Through the soundproof glass, I saw Wally and his companions in the control room laughing, sipping coffee. My audition was over.

"Next," shouted a script assistant who waved in the young woman I'd met in line who was auditioning for the role of Lady Jaye—Flint's love interest in the show.

A week after my audition, my voiceover agent called.

"You got the role as Flint," she said.

I thought, *Okay, it's a day's work and a few hundred dollars in my pocket for standing at a microphone barking out military commands.*

I had no idea that being cast as the voice of Flint would turn out to be the biggest stroke of show business luck I would experience in my career.

I worked on *G.I. Joe* for two years in over fifty episodes. Flint even appeared in a few episodes of *Transformers*. We recorded in large groups in order to achieve the feeling of an ensemble. Playing Flint was a fun day at work.

I watched G.I. Joe become an immensely successful toy merchandising vehicle for Hasbro. Today, the G.I. Joe marketing campaign serves as the business model for what internet merchandisers hope to achieve with their young audiences. The characters who came to life in *G.I. Joe* planted the seeds of long-lasting brand loyalty in viewers. Kids who watched *G.I. Joe* gather today as adults with their own children at G.I. Joe toy collectors' conventions to trade action figures, reminisce, and meet the voices and creators of their favorite animated *G.I. Joe* characters.

Recently, I was invited to speak at the Hasbro/G.I. Joe Toy Collectors Convention, known to insiders as JoeCon. Hasbro took note of the continued enthusiasm for the G.I. Joe brand and licensed its name to JoeCon, which takes place every year in a different city around the United States and features an annual release of new action figures, a convention floor, booths, guest speakers, seminars, dinners, and most importantly, a place for *G.I. Joe* fans to gather. They have organized websites, fan clubs, podcasts, and online stores selling vintage G.I. Joe action figures, vehicles, and play sets. (Hasbro's *Transformers* fans function similarly in their parallel universe.)

In the lobby of the J.W. Marriott in downtown Indianapolis, dozens of men and women gathered, many wearing battle fatigues. Voice actress Mary MacDonald-Lewis who played Flint's love interest, Lady Jaye, was there, looking exactly as her character had looked in the TV cartoon—military-style boots, olive-drab shirt with epaulettes, and a short, attractive, no-nonsense brunette hair-do. Mary and I were flown in as invited guests at JoeCon where we were scheduled to sign autographs, deliver seminars, and mingle with *G.I. Joe* fans for the two-day convention. Over the years I had received invitations from other *G.I. Joe* events, but I was hesitant to leave my voiceover clients in order to attend a toy convention. I had no idea what I was in for.

In the hotel lobby, I spotted Lady Jaye talking with fans. Mary and I have known each other since we met in line at the G.I. Joe auditions in the early 1980s, and we have watched each other's kids grow up. Lady Jaye and I greeted each other and hugged. A hush fell over the room. Dozens of adults dressed in camouflage gear stared in awe. Before their eyes, Lady Jaye and Flint had come to life.

Taking Mary's hand, I announced, "Ladies and gentlemen, the legendary love persists. Yo, Joe!"

Applause broke out. G.I. JoeCon had begun. In addition to Lady Jaye and Flint, JoeCon also invited writer/animator Larry Hama and Hasbro's former Product Manager, Kirk Bozigian—veterans of the TV and toy markets. Throughout the weekend, we moved from the autograph table, to the convention floor, to the dinner table, and had conversations with dozens of Joe fans. I spoke with Iraq and Afghan war vets who had brought their families to JoeCon. Everyone I encountered that weekend was unfailingly kind to me.

The convention floor was crowded with booths selling G.I. Joe t-shirts, posters, vintage collectible action figures in their original packaging, custom hand-built action vehicles, re-purposed action figures that had been painstakingly disassembled and reassembled as militarized Santa Claus figures and assorted uniformed changelings. Scores of fans lined up at the autograph tables and handed us animation cells, cards, illustrations of Flint and Lady Jaye, and unopened packages of vintage and new action figures. We signed autographs for hours. Some fans wanted personalized autographs for their friends and family. Others sold the autographed items on the internet. One man returned to the autograph tables repeatedly with bags of *G.I. Joe* memorabilia. As tactfully as I could, I asked, "Do you sell this stuff on eBay?"

"Yeah, I hope to move all of this stuff next week. It pays the rent."

I was happy to support the man's habit of collecting and selling toys from a TV show that had done so much for my career. Foolishly, I had managed to collect only a few pieces of Joe memorabilia—a poster from the initial mini-series, a few action figures of Flint and Lady Jaye, and a bottle of G.I. Joe shampoo featuring a screw-top Flint head which my daughter gave me for Christmas.

I was deeply touched by the attention and the level of intense loyalty the fans showed me and Mary. I felt a little uncomfortable receiving a degree of attention that I didn't feel I personally deserved. I had to be careful to keep my ego in check and remind myself that it wasn't really me or Mary they were there to see. It was the voices of Flint and Lady Jaye—the characters in the TV show—that were the draw.

At the autograph table, one young man told me, "My wife gets irritated with me because while I help her prepare supper for the kids, I listen to you guys on the soundtracks of my old VHS copies of *G.I. Joe*. I like to listen to your voices."

A man in his forties approached me in the hallway outside the Grand Ballroom before supper on Saturday night. "I just want to thank you for being here for us this weekend and for teaching us how to live."

I was confused. I am not a minister or a guru. I am a cartoon voice actor. I didn't know how to respond.

"What do you mean, 'Teaching us how to live'?" I asked.

"You know, all those G.I. Joe public service announcements Flint appeared in, talking about morality and ethics and stealing and lying and stuff?"

I recalled a *G.I. Joe* recording session at which a producer handed me a handful of thirty-second announcements. "You don't get paid any extra for these," the producer said, "so don't ask. National parent groups have climbed on the anti-*G.I. Joe* bandwagon, so we're having you narrate some *G.I. Joe* Public Service Announcements. They are scenarios like where a kid tosses a baseball through a window, then claims his sister did it. Your character, Flint, drives up in a jeep and tells the kid it's better to tell the truth, kind of like Honest Abe Lincoln."

I read Walt Disney books aloud to my children, and I felt frustrated with the awkward, ham-fisted Disney attempts at moralizing to readers. But the young man who stood before me that day at JoeCon was not being ironic. He meant what he said.

Another fan came up to me and said, "I hope you know that you are directly responsible for a good number of us becoming first-responders and military."

I had no idea the effect that this television show had on a generation of people who watched devotedly every day.

Saturday evening, we were asked to attend the convention supper and to mingle with the guests. In the main ballroom, I sat down with a group of fans, but I avoided mentioning that I was an invited guest. One of my fellow diners said, "Folks, are you aware that you are in the presence of the voice of Flint?"

A hush fell over the table. Trying to deflect some of the focus, I turned to Beverly Perkins, the mother of the young man across the table from me. The young man displayed an encyclopedic knowledge of production details about *G.I. Joe* and many other TV and comic book series.

"Mrs. Perkins, how do you feel about your grownup son being such a *G.I. Joe* expert?"

"Well, my son Troy and I are both school teachers. With the help of Troy's G.I. Joe action figure collection, I've raised the literacy level of my ninth grade English classes."

Barbara Perkins teaches in an inner-city Pittsburg, Pennsylvania, high school. In an effort to raise the reading level of her English class, she brought her son Troy's *G.I. Joe* comic books, DVDs, and action figures into the classroom.

"And my students began to read. I didn't care that they were reading comic books. They were reading. And I had them play imagination games with the action figures. We have *G.I. Joe* Fridays. The literacy rate of my students has gone up by over 50 percent."

I was astounded at Barbara Perkins story. Her method of teaching reading to her ninth-graders utilizing a popular TV cartoon, action figures, and comic books in the classroom was a novel one. This speaks not only to the inventiveness of a dedicated school teacher but also to the power and creativity of child's play.

Later that evening, I sat with former Hasbro Product Manager Kirk Bozigian, who orchestrated Hasbro's spectacularly successful G.I. Joe toy merchandising campaign in the 1980s. We discussed today's computer game companies, and I assumed that they enjoyed the same kind of success with their ancillary toy sales as Hasbro did with its G.I. Joe toy line. Computer and video games are hugely successful.

I was surprised when Bozigian told me, "Gamers don't buy toys. They play the games non-stop. Kids used to watch a single half-hour episode of *G.I. Joe* a day. In order for kids to keep the Joe Team vibe going, they bought the toys and played with them. Not gamers. They're gaming 24/7."

Hearing Bozigian's explanation of kids' online gaming habits and lack of enthusiasm for toys was sobering. It makes *G.I. Joe* seem innocent by comparison. When the gaming industry takes away from children the incentive to engage in creative play, it puts them in a precarious position—sitting at their computers and game consoles, participating in pre-scripted scenarios, staring at a screen.

CHAPTER EIGHT

TV PROMO WORLD

I drove onto the ABC-TV lot in East Hollywood to narrate promotional announcements for the Academy Awards. I was excited; the little kid in me was rubbing his hands together and stomping his feet in glee. Oh, boy, the Oscars. I took my seat in front of a black Sennheiser 416 tube microphone. The promo producer handed me my script. The concrete sound studio called "Post 2" was located in a nondescript one-story beige building behind the gates of the old Prospect Studios lot, once home to Vitagraph Studio where Al Jolson starred in *The Jazz Singer*, America's first talking picture. The promo producer, audio mixer, and the line producer sat in office chairs in front of the audio mixing console with its blinking LEDs, slider pots, and digital switches.

The promo producer stared at me for a moment.

"Wait a minute," he said. "Aren't you the guy who doesn't let your kids watch television?"

"Well, we watch videos and movies together sometimes."

"Let me get this straight. You won't let your kids watch television. But we pay you to tell other people to watch TV?"

"Right. Here's how I see it," I started.

The rest of the crew leaned back in their seats, sensing that a discussion was about to ensue.

"I have two jobs," I told the promo producer. I was vamping. I had never been confronted like this. I tried to sound rational and coherent. "First, I'm a parent, and frankly, I think kids are better off, the less TV they watch. They've got homework."

The producer's face was blank. Either he was bored or he didn't get it.

I continued, "Secondly, I'm an announcer, available to read your promo on the air as long as it doesn't directly advocate debauchery, destruction, or death."

"Well, some of our shows certainly do."

"The Academy Awards?"

"Not directly, no."

Staffers in the room had begun to check their watches. We were on the clock. I didn't really care whether my producer agreed with me or not. I had stated my media philosophy: I'm a voiceover guy for hire, but I'm also a parent.

As a parent, I have qualms about electronic entertainment. As a kid, I loved television. But even then, I knew I watched too much TV. When I was nine years old, my older brother, Pete, attempted to stage an intervention. He dragged me into his bedroom and pointed to his shelf filled with books—*Dr. Doolittle*, *Tom Swift*, *The Hardy Boys Mysteries*.

"You see these? They're called books," he said. "I read them. They make my mind work. You? You're a TV addict. You're hooked on the boob tube. All you do is sit there. You'll end up becoming a moron."

I remained silent. I had no counter-argument. Did his lecture work? Of course not. I kept on watching *Dragnet*, *77 Sunset Strip*, *Gunsmoke*, and the rest of the endless stream of programs the TV networks fed into the pipeline. I am a child of the Television Age.

On my first day of kindergarten, my dad bought us our first television. He hauled the big, ungainly set into the living room and plugged it in.

"Son, twist the knob clockwise like this, wait for it to warm up, and there you go—TV. Don't look at it for too long, though, or your eyes will pop out of your head."

I stared at the dark mahogany cabinet. The screen was shaped like a porthole on a ship. I twisted the knob, and the TV set began to crackle and hiss. After many seconds of waiting, the black-and-white image of a man in railroad engineer's overalls appeared. "I'm Boxcar Bob, and I'll be back with more puppets, cartoons, and other fun stuff right after this message."

Then a disembodied voice came on: "This commercial message will be sixty seconds long." *Sixty seconds.* I held my breath as a brand new Oldsmobile 88 drove across the screen, a happy family of four waving out the window. I ran into the kitchen.

"Mom, I know what a minute is—sixty seconds."

"That's right, honey. Did you learn that in kindergarten?" she asked, brushing potato peelings from her apron.

"No, the man on TV said it."

"Oh, Boxcar Bob?"

"No. This man was invisible."

"Oh," she said. "The announcer."

The announcer . . . the announcer's voice had entered my consciousness—deep and authoritative, calm, dignified, intelligent-sounding. And the hold my parents had on me, my manners, my thoughts, my very development as a human being, they had unwittingly turned over to the idiot box, the glass teat, the vast wasteland of television. I now belonged to the first generation of our species raised by a machine—an RCA Victor seventeen-inch Model 7-T-122.

The next afternoon, I turned the TV on again, and this time it showed a dark hallway inside a dreary downtown boarding house.

Two marionettes dressed as gangsters in black Fedora hats and rumpled suits lurked on either side of an apartment door with their guns drawn. A square-jawed lawman wearing a police badge and a derby hat opened the door. Detective Fearless Fosdick. The bad guys fired their guns. Fearless staggered back and tore open his jacket. His chest was ventilated with smoking bullet holes. Fearless's girlfriend, Eunice Pimpleton, ran into the hallway, followed by their landlady, Mrs. Flintnose. The bad guys hightailed it down the hall. Mrs. Flintnose scowled at the blood on her carpet. Eunice Pimpleton screamed, "Oh, Fearless, Fearless! You've been shot!"

"Only a flesh wound, dear. Don't worry about me. I'm going after the goons who did it." (Cue the mystery music.)

A voice announced, "Tune in next time for another episode of *Fearless Fosdick.*" The dim lights glinted on the puppet strings as Fearless Fosdick and Eunice Pimpleton joined hands and walked down the hallway in that herky-jerky puppet way.

Fearless Fosdick was the first live police procedural show featuring marionettes. Every week for a month, I watched *Fearless Fosdick.* I was hooked. But one week, *Fearless* wasn't on. Instead, they substituted an episode of *The Adventures of Spin and Marty*, starring Tim Considine. NO! I hated *Spin and Marty*. Where was Fearless?

"Dad, *Fearless Fosdick's* not on. What happened?"

My father leaned back in his easy chair.

"Calm down, son. We'll figure it out. Hand me the newspaper. We'll check the TV listings." He scanned the paper and wrinkled his brow. "I'm sorry, kid. It looks like they took *Fearless Fosdick* off the air."

"Off the air?!"

"Son, remember what I'm about to tell you. There is no accounting for quality in television."

My heart sank. I felt a titanic disappointment. "Dad, what does that mean?"

"It means if *Fearless Fosdick* didn't get good ratings, show's over."

"But he's the best thing on TV."

"Son, you and I are for sale. We're TV viewers. And if they can't sell enough of us to the sponsor, they kill the show. You may never see Fearless again. You can blame the sponsors."

But I liked the sponsors. They made all those funny commercials. The sponsors killed Fearless Fosdick? With these few words of wisdom, my father had sown in me a lifelong skepticism of the media—the suspicion that the electronic marketplace doesn't have my interests at heart. And as the so-called "Golden Age of Television" faded and the mass-marketers got a firm grip on TV, my father's warning of creeping mediocrity in electronic entertainment was borne out.

———

Commercial voiceover is a quick in-and-out job. Fewer than half a dozen people come together briefly for a recording session—the ad agency producer, the copywriter, the client, the recording engineer, and the voiceover talent—and often only on the telephone. In less than an hour, it's over. Another product sold, another TV show ballyhooed, another movie promoted. Then it's on to the next gig, the next employer. Voiceover is primarily a commercial art. It is commissioned by the marketplace. With the exception of voice acting in animated projects, voiceovers are words on a page written to be spoken for one purpose—to sell something.

Advertising, consuming, and manufacturing keep our economy moving. Consumers fall under the sway of advertising, they buy things, and factories keep busy. That's life in America. But why wasn't I nostalgic about the good times I'd had on the job—the friendships, the fun of Hollywood and Madison Avenue advertising projects? I thought about this for months. When I perform my job I am not creating a beautiful painting to look at, a luxurious chair for people to sit in, or a comfortable sweater to wear. I'm helping to create a message that urges consumers to consume.

Writer Gertrude Stein said about her hometown of Oakland,

California, "There is no *there* there." I wonder if the same thing could be said of commercials. Though I continue doing voiceovers to this day, my vague sense of emptiness about the commercial marketplace ultimately led me to return to college at age forty-six and create media awareness programs for schoolchildren and to study creative writing. I remember my father referring to some of his ad agency copywriters as "frustrated writers."

"What's a frustrated writer?" I asked.

"Son it's someone who wants to write the great American novel, but instead he writes hairspray commercials."

At television stations, my job is to narrate promotional announcements for the news. Local news programs are the most profitable portion of a TV station's schedule. Stations have to pay for network prime-time shows and syndicated programs like *Dr. Phil* or *Ellen*, but a station produces its own local news shows, sells advertising during the news, and keeps the profits. Stations are staffed with TV promo writers and producers who confer with news editors on the big stories of the day and decide which ones they want to promote to viewers. These promos are meant to convince viewers to "stay tuned" for the upcoming story.

I was on the KABC-TV lot in Los Angeles getting ready to record one such promo for the Five o'clock News. It was New Year's Eve. The lead story was a bloody gang murder at a local theme park, followed by a puff piece about what to wear to a New Year's Eve party.

"*Tonight on the Five o'clock News—murder at a local theme park! We talk with the victims' families. Then, New Year's Eve party gowns! The stores are open! You can still dress up for New Year's, on the cheap! Tonight at five.*"

There was something wrong with this promo. The transition between stories felt insensitive to the murder victims' families. I suggested to the producer that we flip-flop the stories—start with the party dresses and end with the theme park murders. She stared at the promo and shook her head.

"No, just read it the way it's written."

"But don't you think it's disrespectful to the families to tag out their grief with a story about party dresses?"

She looked at the copy again. "Let's just do it the way it is."

She wasn't going to budge. Perhaps she felt like I was criticizing her. And I certainly didn't want her to tell her boss, "The announcer refuses to read the promo."

"Look, I'll read it," I said. "I'm not suggesting you re-write it. Just flip-flop the two stories. It won't sound so creepy."

Again, she looked at the copy and shook her head. Perhaps she felt it would lose impact by doing what I suggested. Maybe she didn't want to end the promo on a downer. The operative philosophy in local TV news is "If it bleeds, it leads." Horror stories attract viewers far more effectively than happy stories, and as a result, we see primarily horror stories on TV news, and those are the stories we remember.

TV stations profit most from their local news programs; consequently, there is up to six hours of local news programming on nearly every local TV station. In case of weather emergencies or catastrophe, local TV news can be quite helpful to viewers. Otherwise, local TV news is usually a smorgasbord of murder, mayhem, accidents, and terrorism. A PBS/SoCal article about local news called "The Ratings Game" says, "Advertisers have conducted research that indicates crime-related stories are interesting to viewers, which increases pressure on news operations to add more of those stories to their nightly lineups."[22]

Studies have shown that the more TV news one watches, the more fearful one is of the world. We've all read headlines like, "Lawyer Says Nine-Year-Old Bank Robber Was Influenced by TV Crime," "Teen Bites 11 People, Blames It on *Twilight*," or "Video Game Addict Killed by Deep Vein Thrombosis." Lenore Skenazy, mother of two, wrote the book, *Free-Range Kids: Giving Our Children the Freedom We Had without Going Nuts with Worry*, in which she says that the media and advertisers are whipping up a national hysteria in parents about child safety in order to sell TV news programs and products.[23]

In fact, despite all the violence and mayhem the news reports, Harvard psychologist Steven Pinker, in his book *The Better Angels of Our Nature: Why Violence Has Declined*, writes that statistics show that we are becoming less violent as a species in the twenty-first century.[24] The real issue is that children are watching way more than just TV, and they are watching too much of it. They may have a TV set in their own bedroom. They have their own smart phones, tablets, laptops, and gaming platforms. An article in the *New York Times* Education section quoted a Kaiser Family Foundation study, "The average young American now spends practically every waking minute—except for the time in school—using a smart phone, computer, television, or other electronic device."[25] What effect does this have on a child's mind? What is it doing to his or her ability to learn, to relate to family and friends, to function in the world?

In the average American home, a television set is on eight hours a day. Even though kids generally don't pay much attention to local TV news, chances are good that your child is seeing at least some of the mayhem on a regular basis. This begs an important question: how closely are you watching what your children watch?

CHAPTER NINE

THE SCORCHING LURE OF THE MEDIA

When I was ten years old I almost burned my house down. Every afternoon, I came home from school and reached into the front hallway closet where the mail arrived through the slot. I was impressed by mail. There was a power to it. If you had the ability to attract as much mail as my father did, you were a powerful person, a mail magnet.

Because my father worked in advertising, our home was filled with magazines and catalogues. We had TVs in our house, but magazines played an equally important role in eliciting in me an early obsession with media. New magazines arrived in the mail every day—*National Geographic, The Saturday Evening Post, Time, Newsweek, Popular Mechanics, Readers Digest, Life, Sports Illustrated, Golf, Radio & TV, The New Yorker. Medical Digest.* I carried magazines and catalogues into the living room and sniffed the ink and stared at glossy photographs of the Himalayas, Canadian winters, and models in ads for clothing, automobiles, and French perfumes.

It was the display ads that drew me in. In my bedroom closet, I hid my private collection of photographs of models. I cut them out of magazines and newspapers and kept them hidden inside a two-foot-long toy metal UPS truck inside a crawlspace behind my bedroom wall. I spent hours in that crawlspace looking at my collection by candlelight—crinkled black and white newsprint lingerie ads featuring the most beautiful women in the world.

Was this appropriate for a ten-year-old? My mother didn't think so. One afternoon, I came home from school and saw my UPS truck on the dining room table. "Billy, let's chat," she said. I had been found out. "I'm not angry, and I'm not going to show these to your father, but these pictures of yours are not appropriate for a ten-year-old."

"Mom, I got that stuff out of the newspaper."

"I know, dear, but all together it's more like what you'd find in a college fraternity, not in a fourth-grader's bedroom."

I got my UPS truck back, but not the photos. My rather lurid collection of display advertisements had created deeply personal, intimate experiences for me with total strangers. With those magazine pages, I began to experience the hypnotic power of the human figure. Due to the allure of photography, and because I was a child with an active imagination, I experienced imaginary relationships with models, movie stars, and public figures. As I perused faces, I would dote on each one, and sometimes I would wonder, *Would she like me?*

"New Elizabeth Arden holds hair in place with a gossamer touch..." *No, not this one. She looks aloof, unfriendly*, and I'd turn the page.

"So fresh! So fragrant! So wonderfully sure! Blue Grass deodorant stick ... " *Oh, maybe this pink-cheeked one. She looks kind, friendly. Do you like me?* I wondered.

Sometimes a particular face would strike my fancy, and I would add her to my photo collection. When I watched television, I found myself searching the faces of actors, hosts, and commercial spokespersons, looking for personal meaning, a relationship—the very thing TV programmers and advertisers hope I will do. This is how the medium fulfills its purpose—to hold you close and sell you things: new clothes, skin cream, crunchy cereal, trips to exotic places. I imagined owning the things I saw in pictures. I began to clip out coupons of all kinds, fill them out with my name and address, and send them in. Soon, I was receiving almost as much mail as my father.

A photograph of Miss Wisconsin appeared one Sunday in the "Style" section of the *Minneapolis Sunday Tribune*. My dad had taught me to read the newspaper, but I didn't really read it so much as stare at the pictures. The photo of Miss Wisconsin took up nearly a quarter-page—large in proportion to the amount of text beneath her picture: "The newly-crowned Miss Wisconsin is Margaret Wells. Hailing from Spider Lake, a friendly farm community south of the Wisconsin Dells, Miss Wells is pictured in her prize-winning swimsuit pose from a recent competition in Milwaukee."

Miss Wisconsin was gorgeous—dark hair, lips that I imagined were ruby red. (It was a black and white photograph.) She wore black high heels and a white tank suit. Her skin was smooth and unblemished. If Veronica of the Archie comic books came alive, this is what she might have looked like. Miss Wisconsin stared at me with her arm lifted behind her head, her hand cradling her neck in theatrical yet relaxed pose.

I put the "Style" section on the dining room table and got a pair of scissors from the kitchen. My parents were reading in the living room. If I was quiet, they wouldn't notice what I was up to. I wouldn't have to answer questions like, "Why are you cutting up the newspaper? We haven't read the 'Style' section yet, Billy. What are you doing?"

I learned by accident that newsprint could be torn in a near-perfect straight line from the top of the page down. If I ripped the page sideways a ragged uneven tear would result. I grabbed my mother's pinking shears and started cutting down the edge of the picture, giving Miss Wisconsin a wide berth, but the heavy metal scissors slipped from my fingers, and the page ripped—a vertical tear along the thin black line that separated Miss Wisconsin from the wedding announcements. I wasn't one of those kids who had gotten the Kindergarten assessment "Very good with scissors." But she was intact. I ran upstairs with her under my arm. Before stuffing her in with the rest of my collection, I took one last look at Miss Wisconsin in her pleated white tank suit and black high heels. Her dark hair and painted lips reminded me of my Aunt Caroline—traditional, yet totally woman.

In the rear corner of my closet was an opening to a narrow, six-foot passage. It led behind the wall to a windowless space the size of a small room. My older brother, Pete, and I shared the third floor of our colonial-style red brick house. In his room, he had one closet. But due to a quirk in the architecture I had three closets. In one, I kept my comic book collection which was heavy on *Archie & Jughead*, *Dennis the Menace*, DC Comics' *Superman and Batman*. The second closet contained my five-watt AM radio station WCLO. I was wired for sound. My brother Pete and his friends often came to my room and made music requests: "Play an Elvis record." "Play *Heartbreak Hotel*." I was the only working DJ they knew.

Inside my third closet, behind my school clothes and blue jeans, was the opening to the crawlspace. To enter I had to kneel down, and, careful to avoid splinters, I dragged myself along the wooden planks into the blackness. It smelled of old pine and creosote. When I reached the end of the short tunnel, I lit a match. Dried plaster oozed from between strips of wooden lath. Yellowed wads of a newspaper stuck out of the wall, filling the gaps between layers of plaster. It struck me as rather irresponsible of workmen to have stuck newspaper into the walls of a wooden house. It could catch fire. It appeared that no one had been inside this crawl space since the house was built in 1925. I was the only one in my family who knew about it. I felt powerful and perfectly alone.

"Billy."

Through the wall came the muffled voice of my mother.

"Billy, we've got to go shopping for school clothes."

I blew out the match. The blackness absorbed the sounds of my breathing.

"Come on, I know you're in there. I heard you. Billy? Come out of there."

I sat still and said nothing. Finally I heard the sound of my mother walking back downstairs. I lit another match and touched it to the wick of a Christmas choirboy candle I had saved from the holidays. As the candlewick burned at the top of the choirboy's head, a drop of wax flowed down his white and red Ecclesiastical garb. The candle shed plenty of light—enough to illuminate Miss Wisconsin's torso. She lay on the floor, folded and creased. I didn't want to smooth her out. I was afraid she might tear. In the candlelight, she looked distort-ed, not as pretty as before. I watched as the wax from the choirboy candle flowed down onto the floor and disappeared between the floorboards.

Suddenly the floor was on fire. In a panic, I scrambled out of the crawl space and got a cup of water from the bathroom. I crawled back in and tossed the water on the floor. It kept burning. I remembered the Smokey the Bear cartoon on TV where Smokey said, "You, too, can prevent forest fires," as he beat out a campfire with a blanket. I was wearing my brother's brand-new Minnesota Gophers sweatshirt. I pulled it over my head and swung it at the fire over and over, soaking my brother's favorite garment with candle wax. The fire went out.

Luckily, Miss Wisconsin was unharmed. My spirits, however, had been dampened. The crawlspace was full of smoke. I had nearly burned my house down. I lifted the metal roof off my UPS truck and carefully put Miss Wisconsin back in with the rest of my collection. I crawled back out, exited my room, and went downstairs.

"Where were you?" asked my mother.

"I was storing stuff." My mind raced to come up with a credible reason for why I hadn't answered her when she called my name. "And

I had headphones on. I was listening to my transistor radio." I don't think she believed me.

Today as an adult I receive plenty of magazines and catalogues, and embarrassing as it is to admit, I still stare at the models. And they still come alive for me. I attribute this to the hypnotic power of commercial photography. Photos of catalogue models and celebrities are specifically designed to to involve you, to pull you close. The next time you see a copy of *Vanity Fair* or *Us* or *People* or your L. L. Bean catalogue, take a close look at the faces. They're looking at you, aren't they? Of course, they're actually looking at the camera. But the purpose of the photo is to make you feel that they are looking directly at you. And so it goes with advertising in any medium, from billboards to pop-up ads on your smart phone. You are supposed to feel close to the subjects. And the closer we feel, the closer we are to opening up our wallets and buying whatever is that our special friends are selling. And for a child, this is rather dangerous. I was primed to buy anything the electronic marketplace wanted to sell me. Lucky for me, there was no internet back then for me to stare at day in and day out.

If I had gone on to become a commercial photographer, I could claim that my time spent tucked away inside a stuffy crawlspace staring at magazine photographs was well worth it. But looking back, I think my time would have been better spent out on the ball field.

———

In the 1980s, I hosted a morning radio show on KBIG/Los Angeles FM 104. I was always looking for stories. I attended the twentieth anniversary of Marilyn Monroe's death at the Westwood Cemetery near the UCLA campus, not far from the rather modest bungalow where Marilyn was found dead of a drug overdose on August 5, 1962. At the cemetery, there was a crowd, some dressed in mourning garb, black gowns, and long veils. There were limos with actresses—or pretend actresses, it was hard to tell—stepping out onto the cemetery drive in shiny black pumps, holding a handkerchief to their breasts. A man dressed as a minister began a graveside service, although there was no grave per se. Marilyn's remains had been placed in a pilaster niche behind a white veined marble plaque with her name and birth and death dates.

A man stood on the grass beside me with a large shopping bag filled with framed photographs of Marilyn. I'd been in Hollywood for only a few years, so naïvely I thought this man must have been a friend or at least a member of the crew on her movies at Twentieth Century Fox.

"Did you work with Marilyn?" I asked.

"Oh, no, I wish I had. I just have so much respect for her."

"You have a lot of photos of her."

"Yes, I brought some of them with me today. There are so many, I had to leave the rest at home."

I pictured this modest-looking fellow sitting in his apartment somewhere in the vast Los Angeles Basin surrounded by dozens of framed photographs of Marilyn Monroe—purchased at memorabilia shops on Hollywood Boulevard or torn from the pages of *Modern Screen*, *Photoplay*, or *Life Magazine*. This reminded me of my meager collection of photos I kept hidden away in my crawlspace behind my childhood bedroom closet. Though I had not been obsessed with movie stars (I was simply interested in women in general), it occurred to me that this was the same thing, really. This unassuming man in khaki pants and shirt sleeves who had brought part of his collection of photographic totems was practicing a sophisticated version of what I did as an eight-year-old. This collector of Marilyn images had invented a relationship.

He didn't know Marilyn in the real world. But in his imagination, Marilyn Monroe took center stage, and though I couldn't see into his apartment—perhaps he had a smaller shrine of photographs dedicated to his mother—in his world, the most important thing was his love for Marilyn. His photos of her, which he had lovingly framed and then packed up and brought to her grave in a shopping bag on the twentieth anniversary of her death, were his conduit to intense emotion—loyalty, love, dedication, obsession. Was he a dangerous person? Probably not. He didn't appear to be insane, only obsessed with a dead movie star.

We look at photos of famous people, we watch them on our assorted devices, and we feel emotionally connected to complete strangers. Video gamers feel connected to animated characters who skulk through dark landscapes looking for foes to vanquish or cars to steal. Is this any different from ancient religions where men and women worshipped animals of the wild and spirits who they believed held the power of the wind and the sun? What is different today is that profit-seeking global corporations are carefully arranging these encounters for us with the objects of our fascination. We buy an array of electronic devices through which we can dream of love, loyalty, honor, conflict, fear, escape, capture, dominance, and consumption— all with beautiful, powerful-looking beings who are not part of our lives in any way except through our screens.

This is modern entertainment. This is advertising. This is the internet with its endless library of video imagery that would take us a million lifetimes to watch, with its clunky pop-up ads, often featuring scantily clad people who beckon us to click through and deposit a drop of our personal data. We've always been fascinated by the human figure. We stroll in public spaces and stare at each other. In museums, we look at statuary, paintings, videos, and films. In the commercial marketplace, which has worked its way inside our homes in so many ways (great-grandma and great-grandpa used to have only a few magazines, the newspaper, and a radio), billions of dollars are spent arranging actors and models to look like our friends, our families, our dreams.

Today, electronic entertainment is America's most successful export. And watching it is the one activity we spend our greatest amount of time doing other than sleeping. Some of it is wonderful amusement. But its very reason for being, the one thing that under-writes it and justifies its existence, is its ability to sell you and your children an endless stream of products and services—whether you need them or not. And along the way, with help from the world's most sophisticated consumer surveillance system, it learns and stores your buying and consuming habits in order to sell you more. There are probably terabytes of my family's online shopping history stored on a server somewhere west of the Great Divide.

Every year, my family and I watch the Academy Awards (also known as the Oscars) together. As always, The Oscars 2014 was a combination of vaguely funny jokes, mediocre dance numbers, and teary-eyed acceptance speeches.

As the hosts who have come before her, Ellen DeGeneres bravely attempted to tame the unwieldy beast that is the three-and-a-half-hour Oscars telecast. To amuse the crowd, Ellen ordered pizza and fed it to the stars on-camera as a billion viewers around the world looked on. In an effective on-camera product placement coup by Oscars sponsor Samsung, Ellen wandered the aisles of the Dolby Theater snapping selfies with celebrities using a Samsung smart phone. (Ellen was later seen backstage tweeting on her own Apple iPhone, having abandoned the larger and more unwieldy Samsung.)

None these buddying-up–to-the-stars bits were particularly funny, but they did achieve something that the Oscars seldom do. They showed the stars to be human. Celebrities fumbled in their pockets for change to pay the pizza man who stood at the apron of the stage. They made funny faces as they posed for Ellen's camera, just as we all do with our friends and family. I found myself somehow being drawn to these distant celebrities. I savored the casual on-camera moments between members of Hollywood's reigning royalty. The rational side of me dismissed this as nothing more than effective manipulation of the audience by a savvy TV network awards show. But the emotional side of me felt, *Gosh, the stars are human just like us.* I felt oddly close to them.

Though I am a somewhat cynical, experienced media worker, I was sucked in just like any other fan. I had fallen for the dumb show. I don't mean "dumb" as in stupid or senseless. In medieval times, the dumb show was a dramatic scene played without words by actors on stage, using only gestures and pantomime, portraying everything from a worried mother cradling a sick child in her arms to an errant clown making fun of a pompous rival. The Oscars' manipulative brilliance is at the root of all that is successful about modern electronic media. What we see on TV, in movies, on our gaming platforms, smart TVs, and iPads, appears far more sophisticated than the open-air stages of fifteenth century Europe, but the idea is the same. An audience gathers to watch performers play at being characters who elicit an emotional response from us. We are seduced by hand puppets in a *Punch & Judy* show, action heroes in a game, and by skilled actors and presenters—all for the same purpose: to earn our money and sell snacks, drinks, and products—in person or by sophisticated digital delivery systems. And the result is the same: after the show, you've been seduced, made to laugh and cry by professional entertainers, and your wallet is just a bit lighter.

The morning after the Oscars, I leafed through the *Los Angeles Times*, hoping to milk a few more drops of show business magic from the previous night's TV event. Perhaps I wanted to feel more connected to the stars whom I watched pose, mug, emote, and shed tears. Brad Pitt and Angelina Jolie, arguably two of the biggest stars in the Hollywood galaxy, had a very good night at the Oscars. As I looked at the photos in the newspaper, I remembered the gentle on-camera kiss Brad gave Angelina as she rose from her seat to accept her award, and a tear came to my eye. As a self-anointed media expert and advertising professional, how could I, of all people, feel a catch in my throat for super-celebrities—denizens of Hollywood's modern-day Mount Olympus? Sitting at my kitchen table I realized, I am no different from the housewife in Thief River Falls, Wisconsin, who has a tear in her eye as she watches an intimate moment between the stars on TV.

Television is powerful stuff. It sucked me right in. I'm not embarrassed about feeling admiration for humanitarian efforts, but this goes beyond that. What I experienced while watching the Oscars and reading about it the next morning was the illusion of personal closeness with the stars, an emotional yearning, a kinship with people who, for all practical purposes, exist only on-screen—ciphers, shadows. Yet I was drawn to them. I felt as though I wanted them to be my friends. There is a part of me that, while watching television, suspends disbelief—something which actors since time immemorial have been asking of their audiences. Enter my theater and suspend disbelief. Come along on a magical journey, and through me, the performer, you will experience new sensations and see the world in a different light.

The way in which Twenty-first-century-style celebrity is reported—from *NBC Nightly News* to TMZ.com to Twitter, from the obsessive celebrity blogosphere to the popular supermarket slicks and tabloids—offers viewers and readers nothing of any real value. Young, handsome, honey-voiced English TV and film star Benedict Cumberbatch has no idea why people are so interested in his celebrity. A reporter wrote, "There are people out there these days who so love to hear Cumberbatch talk—who so love to watch Cumberbatch exist—that they do not care what he does, as long as they get to observe him doing it."[26]

Today's celebrities are pale imitations of the vast assortment of gods and goddesses of the Classical Age. Joseph Campbell writes in *Power of Myth*: "One of the many distinctions between the celebrity and the hero is that one lives only for self while the other acts to redeem society."[27] In ancient times, mankind's heroes were held up as icons because they had intrinsic value. Contemporary philosopher Alain de Botton writes, "The ancient city-state of Athens was unembarrassed about the act of admiration." Statues were carved and festivals were named after a range of exceptional people like Pericles and Demosthenes, as well as a host of Greek gods and goddesses who were worshipped for their moral qualities. For nearly two thousand years, Roman Catholics and Eastern Orthodox have been worshipping saints and martyrs for their moral virtues. Author Alain De Botton states, "What underlies both the Christian and Athenian approaches to celebrity is a commitment to the idea of self-improvement, as well as the belief that it is via immersion in the lives of great exemplars that we stand the richest chance of learning how to become better versions of ourselves."[28]

By contrast, the contemporary obsession with Brad and Angelina, Lindsay Lohan, Alec Baldwin, Kim Kardashian, and the other paparazzi-plagued gods and goddesses of our digital era offers far less. Contemporary celebrity journalism and its star-hungry audiences appear to want only news of what celebrities wear, how much weight they've gained or lost, whom they've dissed on Twitter, and details about the cracks in their marriages. It's an obsession without much payoff. And thanks to new technology, it's available to us and our children 24/7 in a thousand different ways. In the precious few hours that comprise a childhood, if children are seduced into spending time staring at commercials, celebrities, and virtual worlds of animated game bullies, they will experience less of life itself. Philosopher Eckhart Tolle writes in *The Power of Now*, "Realize deeply that the present moment is all you have."[29]

CHAPTER TEN

CYBER MANNERS

I felt like a thief, but I was determined to find out what had upset my twelve-year-old daughter, Arianna. From the little I could get out of her, I surmised that something had happened in an iChat between my daughter, a girlfriend, and a pair of twelve-year-old boys. So, after my wife took the girls to a movie, I snuck into my daughter's bedroom, powered up her laptop, clicked on the inviting blue iChat speech bubble icon, and hit print. Out came a seven-page transcription of an iChat dialogue between my daughter and her friend on one end, and two boys on the other, all of whom were well-acquainted with each other from our babysitting co-op.

What struck me immediately about this web interchange between twelve-year-olds was its sexual nature and sophistication. This same "conversation" could have taken place inside a college fraternity house. Yet these were sixth-graders.

Instant message platforms like iChat make it clear who says what as each comment is labeled with the name of its sender. I was somewhat relieved to see that the girls were far less sexually provocative than the boys. The boys' comments were aggressive and prurient. They wrote things in iChat that they never would have had the courage to say in person, or even in a telephone conversation. Somehow, the distance and anonymity of the internet had empowered them to say "dirty" things to the girls.

The girls' iChat behavior was coy and somewhat evasive, but they didn't shy away, and they were in deeper than they ever would have been in person or on the phone. The internet had empowered these twelve-year-olds to venture beyond their comfort zones and to enter territory that was far more "adult" than the usual young adolescent boy-girl conversations.

Because of the rather shocking nature of the sexual comments made in my daughter's adolescent iChat, my wife and I brought the subject up to the other parents. None of them were terribly upset or surprised. However, we were all concerned with the aggressive and graphic nature of the boys' comments; and we noted that the girls didn't appear to discourage the boys. The girls were just more indirect. Other than a good talking-to about cyber-manners, we let our twelve-year-olds off the hook.

But the sixteen-year-old girl from our nearby high school, whom I'll call "Kiki," who used a false name to create social media pages and email addresses in order to harass an ex-friend, didn't get off so easily. The perpetrator, Kiki, was a bright, attractive, well-liked girl from an upper-middle-class suburban home. As most sixteen-year-olds will do, Kiki got into a disagreement with a friend at school over a minor issue. A psychologist friend once told me, "At the risk of sounding sexist, studies show that young females, who are ultimately more responsible for family and child-rearing than males, engage in testing the boundaries of communication with their friends during adolescence. All adolescents can be emotional, but girls tend to be more verbal and will push and prod each other and engage in negative conversation for the purpose of finding where the limits are." Interpersonal spats, while often painful, can generally be resolved with the help of a sensitive parent, teacher, or school counselor. But in Kiki's case, her bullying was on the internet; it was untraceable, so there was no mediating force, and ultimately, police and lawyers were brought in.

Kiki had grown tired of her friend "Essie." She felt that Essie had become needy and clingy, and Kiki wanted to end the friendship. But she didn't know how to do it without emotional risk. Then she learned that is was easy to set up fake Facebook and Twitter pages and email addresses. So she created an alternate cyber-identity using a false name. She was no longer "Kiki." She became "Candi." And Candi was a much crueler girl than Kiki ever was.

Candi "friended" Essie on Facebook. Essie accepted the new "friend" request. "Candi" followed Essie on Twitter. Essie followed her back, and a new cyber-friendship was born. But this friendship turned dark and cruel very quickly, for Candi never intended to be Essie's "friend"—cyber or real—but only to hurt her. Candi posted false rumors on the internet about everything from Essie's eating habits to her sex life. She mocked Essie's body type. Whatever way Candi could scurrilously attack Essie, she did. And it hurt.

Adolescents often have hundreds of Facebook "friends" and Twitter followers, and Candi made sure that every one of them learned of Essie's alleged faults. False rumors about Essie were retweeted, and Candi emailed links, connecting others to Essie's Facebook page. This unwanted, anonymous, and insulting internet attention had its intended effect. Essie was humiliated. She was taunted in school by friends and strangers who confronted her with the false internet rumors that Candi was spreading.

Essie and her parents contacted the police and hired an attorney. But, unfortunately, they accused the wrong person. The day local police officers entered the high school, a mutual friend of both Essie and Kiki's was brought into the principal's office for questioning and was accused of cyberbullying Essie. The girl was threatened with expulsion from school.

The real perpetrator, Kiki/Candi, was worried. She watched as an innocent classmate was accused of the misdeeds that she herself had committed. Kiki went to her father, an attorney, and tearfully confessed what she had done. Her father contacted the high school and brought his daughter in to face the consequences. Kiki admitted to school and police officials that she had cyberbullied Essie. Kiki was thanked for her honesty, but she was expelled from school for the cruel nature of the cyberbullying she had perpetrated upon her old friend Essie.

Kiki's parents placed Kiki in a rehabilitation group for school bullies and bullying victims, and they eventually found a school that would accept Kiki as a student. Perhaps time does heal all wounds, but it took years before the high school hallways stopped echoing with the cruel and false rumors that Kiki had ascribed to Essie. For the students, teachers, and parents who were witness to this unfortunate case, the involvement of law enforcement and attorneys and the sad finality of Kiki's expulsion from school shed a new and sobering light on the issue of cyberbullying. Tragically, some victims of cyberbullying have chosen suicide as a way out of their hurt and humiliation. Fortunately, Essie did not attempt suicide. But Kiki's anonymous cyberbullying left a scar on an entire school community.

Being anonymous on the web is all too easy. And it appears that internet anonymity sometimes brings out the worst in people. For this reason, many internet news outlets are now banning anonymous comments from their websites. I believe that most of the angry, taunting comments we see on web pages are comments that the writers would never make if their identities were known.

Is there a solution to this growing problem of cyberbullying? Have you noticed prolonged trouble between your child and others? Are there signs that your child is bullying or being bullied? While previous generations' playground bullies may have left a black eye and swollen lip, cyberbullying leaves scars that aren't always easy to spot. The best thing we can do is talk with our children about their cyber-relationships and make them aware of both the dangers and the temptations.

To prevent cyberbullying, should parents monitor the use of their children's computers and smart phones? Should we regularly check their browsing histories? These are very personal decisions and ones that should be informed by an open and honest dialogue with your children.

CHAPTER ELEVEN

OKAY, I'LL BE HONEST

I believe that television and the assorted electronic screens that surround our children are sophisticated inventions that come to our doorsteps with starkly conflicting agendas. The creative artists who animate and program computer games, and the writers, directors, musicians, composers, editors, and actors in movies, TV shows, and webisodes, call their work "storytelling." The advertising agencies which sell it all to you describe their products as "cutting-edge," "truly useful," and "life-changing." However, the vast cadre of powerful media executives who run Google, Apple, Facebook, Disney, Viacom, etc., call their work "profit maximization."

Can you really have it both ways? The companies that sell us our digital technology and programming obviously can. But can we? In an article published in *The Atlantic Monthly* entitled, "Is Google Making Us Stupid?" Nicholas Carr warned:

> Most of the proprietors of the commercial Internet have a financial stake in collecting the crumbs of data we leave behind as we flit from link to link—the more crumbs, the better. The last thing these companies want is to encourage

leisurely reading or slow, concentrated thought. It's in their economic interest to drive us to distraction.

Today, the richest, most powerful corporations in the world are jockeying for access and media primacy, and their victories depend upon winning the hearts and minds of you and your children. As a parent, you are up against the collective wisdom of the world's most effective marketers and merchandisers, whose sole aim is to score more viewers, clicks, and numbers. Is your family at a disadvantage in this struggle for your loyalty? Do media companies have your interest at heart? They say they do, but what's at stake for them is the bottom line. Take Lehman Brothers, for example—the massive global investment firm that nearly toppled the world economy in 2008 and which was heavily invested in media corporations—advertised a hopeful message to TV viewers not long before the biggest recession since the Great Depression. Their commercial simply said, "You can get there from here." Yes, but where?

I believe that occasionally TV shows and movies can be wonderful and inspiring and can contribute to our lives. I believe that the internet is a tremendously handy source of information and amusement for students, writers, and the everyday web surfer. I believe that screen time in moderate doses can be a relatively harmless and a relaxing time for children and can give them respite from the worries and stresses of school life and complex social relations with peers and family. I believe that Steve Jobs was a genius and was truly inspired by what would make people happy and give us better access to our photographs, our music, and our data. I believe he was inspired by what looked "cool" and was user-friendly. But he was also a corporate CEO and major Apple shareholder, which made him beholden to share-price.

America was built on the shoulders of inventors. We have always been fascinated by what's new. But not everything that has come along and grown popular in our culture has done us much good. Tail fins on American automobiles in the 1950s, iconic in design, proved to be fatal to thousands of young bicyclists and were done away with in short order. The pesticide DDT, invented in 1939, was once touted as a life-saver for farmers, allowing crops to come to market and keeping prices lower for consumers. I used to ride my bicycle behind the local DDT truck every summer in South Minneapolis as it sprayed magical-looking clouds to kill mosquitoes. And DDT was dropped into nearby Lake Harriet to kill the fast-growing underwater weeds and algae that clogged our beaches. I often got a rash after swimming in that lake in the summer. DDT is now known to be a deadly carcinogenic substance that is banned around the world.

Will we discover that being wired up to the internet 24/7 is deadly? Of course not. If there is damage, it won't be so obvious. UCLA's Gary Small, MD, says, "You have young people whose brains are not fully developed. So how a young person chooses to spend their time will have a profound effect on what their brain will be like for the rest of their lives."[30]

Am I at risk? Is my family at risk? Most of us waste time noodling about in the internet. And looking back, I believe I watched way too many shoot-'em-ups on TV as a child. My dad was a big fan of Zane Grey novels, and he and I watched westerns on TV—*Gunsmoke, Bonanza, Have Gun, Will Travel, The Virginian*, and more. And today, in addition to the highfalutin foreign and indy movies my wife and I choose to see, we've also seen every one of the *Fast and Furious* movies. I'm hooked on action. And I honestly believe that a lifetime of watching bang-bang-shoot-'em-dead movies and TV shows has made me a more fearful person. I take more than the proper precautions in life. Perhaps it's a legacy of being a cautious parent. My wife and daughters call me "The Jailer" for the way I am constantly locking doors. I've accidentally locked my family out of the house more than once.

Barbara J. Wilson of the University of Illinois writes on Futureof-Children.org—a project of Princeton University and the Brookings Institute—"Evidence is growing that the fear induced in children by the media is sometimes severe and long-lasting. A survey of more than two thousand elementary and middle-school children revealed that heavy television viewing was associated with self-reported symptoms of anxiety, depression, and post-traumatic stress."[31]

I believe that the plethora of electronic screens available to our children is highly addictive. I believe that if children are allowed to make their own decisions regarding screen time without intervention from their parents, the vast majority will choose the passive role of a watcher. I believe that very few of the qualities we hope for in our children are nurtured by screen time.

I believe that parents and educators can and should control children's access to media screens by the imposition of rules and limits. I believe that a constructive and workable strategy to deal with electronic media in our families starts with conversation in the home. When you include your children in the decision-making process, they take ownership of the issues and tactics.

You can negotiate cellphone-free hours at home, web-free spaces in the house, TV-free portions of the week. During the floods and storms of Hurricane Sandy on the East Coast, many families were screen-free—some for weeks at a time. They coped well, and many reported reading together as a family for the first time. During a recent severe windstorm near our house, we had a three-day electric outage. We all got more reading done in those three days than we ever had before, even if it was by candle light.

I believe that children are willful, intelligent beings who want to be a part of the decision-making in your home. They have opinions. They are familiar with much of what we're discussing in these pages. They are familiar with kids who are game-addicts, text-aholics, and Facebook freaks. Use the wisdom of your kids to help knit together a strategy to deal with the media screens in your home. We've all heard the phrase, "Life is a negotiation." So is parenting, especially when it comes to imposing rules and limits in the wired world which your kids may be much more familiar with than you are.

PART II
SOLUTIONS

By this point in the book, I hope you don't feel that the world is a much bleaker place than you thought. When it comes to technology and kids, I don't believe in averting my eyes. By knowing what we're dealing with and understanding where children's electronic entertainment and advertising comes from and why it's so powerfully addictive and time-consuming, families can navigate today's complex world of technology and the multiplicity of screens and entertainment alternatives in a much smarter way.

In this section, you'll learn how to keep your family up-to-date and engaged while keeping your children safe in a high-tech world. Today's richest corporations are competing on a highly sophisticated playing field, and one of their most important goals is to score your children's hearts and minds through advertising. Studies show that once a child's loyalty is won, he'll be a loyal brand consumer for life. I hope the information and stories in the following chapters will provide you with real-world solutions to the problems of parenting for the digital age.

You'll learn how to keep your family up-to-date and engaged while keeping your children safe in a high-tech world where today's richest corporations are competing on a highly sophisticated playing field. The goal: your children's hearts and minds. Please use the information contained in the following chapters and enjoy the stories. They will provide you with real-world solutions to the problems of parenting for the digital age.

CHAPTER TWELVE

HOW TO START A BABYSITTING CO-OP

"Hello, I'm Junior's mom, and this is Junior. He's potty-trained, and he's had his supper. Bye-bye, Junior. Have fun!"

The woman left three-year-old Junior standing in our friends' entryway clutching his backpack with the most terrified look on his face. Our friends were members of a babysitting co-operative that boasted a roster of sixty families who earned credits by babysitting for each other. It was big and felt impersonal. This childcare model was not for us. We needed babysitting, but not with strangers.

Although my wife is not what you would call a "joiner," after the birth of our first child she searched out neighborhood baby groups. Spending day after day alone with a baby is not good for you or the baby. So every week, we attended a play group that met in the municipal park near our home. We also went to a baby music group taught by a local school teacher and an infant group run by a retired early child education expert. We showed up at an endless stream of baby birthday parties where hot dogs and lemonade were plentiful and where parent networking takes place. Our toddler's social life was busier than ours had ever been.

The downside of all this? My wife and I hadn't been on a proper date alone together in a year and a half. The one thing missing from our lives was babysitting. So we decided to invite a half-dozen couples over whom we'd met through our assorted baby groups to discuss the possibility of forming a babysitting co-op. Some parents were skeptical:

"My child would never go to sleep without me."

"My kid stays up later than other children."

"My child won't let anyone but me brush his teeth."

To our disappointment, the collective fears of the group appeared to outweigh the positives, so we said goodnight to our friends without having started a babysitting group.

Another year went by, and I attended more baby groups with my wife and daughter. I was having some of the sweetest times of my life witnessing my child go through the magic of growth and development, seeing her learn to walk and dance, watching her learn to share, observing her drink from her sippy cup and not spill juice on her new jumper. At these groups my wife and I formed friendships with other parents. We learned that most of these couples had not had a proper night out in a long time. Four of the families had children the same age as our firstborn—two and a half. The two girls were potty trained. The boys were not. Were we up to the challenge?

Children don't come with instruction manuals. Not so long ago, a typical family consisted of aunts, uncles, cousins, and grandparents who would take you aside and tell you how it goes with new babies, toddler tantrums, the difficult questions kids ask, etc. Today, in our mobile society, a family with a baby is lucky if there are any relatives in town willing to help. When I see a lone mother wheeling her child in a stroller, I often wonder, *Why is she alone? Does she have help? Does she have friends with babies? Is she going to go back to work in a few weeks? If so, who's going to take care of her child?* I can only imagine the numbing aloneness of raising a child without friends and family around to pitch in on a regular basis.

At a certain point, our daughter reached the age when we stopped counting in weeks and months, and said instead, "Oh, she's two and a half now." We still hadn't hired a babysitter. The time with our first-born child was precious, and we weren't comfortable entrusting her to a teenage babysitter with questionable childcare skills. We had observed cost-free babysitting groups in operation, but we wanted babysitting from people whom we knew and trusted. But we ached for a night out—to see a movie, have a leisurely supper again, spend time together without the interruptions that occur at home with a toddler. It was time. Four families met again at our house, and this time we were able to put together a babysitting co-operative.

Our small group decided to babysit for each other on Saturday nights from 6:00 p.m. to midnight. We exchanged medical insurance information in case it was ever necessary to take a child for medical help. The host parents would fix supper for the kids, supervise play time and the watching of a video, brush the kids' teeth, get them into their pajamas and sleeping bags, and at a decent hour, read them to sleep with a book.

My wife and I volunteered to create the calendar and babysit the first Saturday, followed by family B, then family C, etc. Every four weeks, my wife and I would host the co-op. The pay-off for us was three consecutive Saturday nights out—a date with my wife, a quiet supper out, a movie, maybe even a double-feature. What a concept!

Our first Saturday night on duty as babysitters worked like clock-work, diaper changing for the boys notwithstanding. As the co-op parents disappeared down our steps for their Saturday night out, their children wailed hysterically, but as soon as the grownups were out of sight, the kids stopped crying and headed for our family room which was filled with toys. What amazed me from the beginning was how self-sufficient young children can be. They don't need to be told how to play. It's instinctual. During playtime, my wife and I simply sat back and watched.

Suppertime came off without a hitch. Even the plastic drop cloths on the kitchen floor proved to be unnecessary. Then came the video. The parents discussed this, and we all agreed that placing the kids in front of a movie for ninety minutes wouldn't undermine our parenting efforts. It wasn't as if we were giving them free reign over hours of unsupervised television viewing. Once the video ended, we turned the TV off, and it was time to brush teeth.

At bed time, the kids took complete ownership of the experience. They each brought their own familiar backpack, sleeping bag, toothbrush, and pajamas, and they handled their belongings with the confidence I would expect from much older children. Before the first night of co-op, I had never brushed another child's teeth besides my own daughter's. But when two-and-a-half-year-old Dexter handed me his Sesame Street toothbrush and toothpaste, I lifted him up, placed him standing on the bathroom tile counter, and brushed his teeth—no muss, no fuss. And soon the co-op kids were peeking out from their sleeping bags, ready for me to read them a book. I thought back to the nights when my father read to me as a child. Magical memories came to mind.

My daughter shouted out, "*Goodnight Moon*, Daddy! Read *Goodnight Moon!*"

"Yeah!" cried the others enthusiastically, as if they were cheering for the LA Dodgers.

As I read—improvising a bit of dialogue, since *Goodnight Moon* is notably short on words—the children were mesmerized by the dreamy mood of the book. But when I finished, all four kids were still wide awake. So I grabbed another title and began to read, but this time I slowed down and allowed my voice to relax. I would lull them to sleep. It worked. Gentle toddler snores emitted from the sleeping bags, and I faded down the lights. My wife and I had two quiet hours before parents would arrive to pick up their sleeping children. Our babysitting co-op was a success.

I took on the scheduling chores for the co-op, making the occasional adjustment or trade when necessary. For three years, our families babysat for each other every week—nearly one hundred fifty Saturday nights of safe, cozy, cost-free babysitting.

Then the co-op kids turned six, and electronic game platforms came on the scene. One Saturday night, Gabe and Dexter both appeared for co-op clutching brand new handheld electronic games. And it all nearly came crashing down. Before supper, the two girls, Nina and Arianna, were playing make believe at the toy plastic sink in our family room. Dexter and Gabe reached into their backpacks and pulled out their new game consoles.

The co-op parents had discussed everything from medical insurance to our kids' favorite brands of toothpaste. But we hadn't discussed what to do with personal electronics. Dexter was the first to fire up his handheld Nintendo. In the kitchen, my wife and I heard beeping and whirring sounds coming from the family room. Then the brawl began.

"Mine! It's MINE! GIVE ME MY GAMEBOY!" shouted six-year-old Dexter as the girls wrestled him to the floor, prying his Nintendo from his sweaty little hands.

Over the years, my wife and I had observed families sitting together in public while their children stared at their handheld game screens. The first time our daughter Arianna asked for a portable game console, I had a visceral and immediate reaction. We were waiting to board an airplane when Arianna noticed numerous children in the airport lounge absorbed in their hand-held electronic games.

"Daddy, I want one of those? Can I have one of those?" asked my daughter.

Precious memories flashed before me—carrying my child on my shoulders, talking happily together, reading to her before bedtime.

I was afraid this would all go away and be replaced by the accursed beeping of a Gameboy. So I said, "No."

"No, what?" she replied, somewhat puzzled.

"No, you can't have a game console."

"Why not?"

My wife whispered, "Can't she have one, just maybe part-time?"

"No," I thundered.

"Shhhh, Daddy, people are staring at you."

"Sorry. But, no."

"Why."

"Because it rots your brain."

"No, it doesn't. Those kids' brains aren't rotten," she said, gesturing at the children in the airport waiting area, busily punching buttons on their game consoles.

I did not want to bring into our lives what I felt was a silly, plastic, noise-making, virtual-play monster whose sole effect would be to divert my child from the world. Yes, it might allow me to watch more football on TV. But kids grow up fast. Once their childhood is gone, you can't get it back. That's the way I felt. So, no Gameboy.

My daughter ultimately didn't seem to care much. And it was the same way for our second child when she reached electronic game platform age. I said, "No," to allowing my children to spend their free time staring at game screens. Do I feel in hindsight that I was a little too harsh? Did I deprive my children of precious, carefree alone time? Was I too doctrinaire, too anti-fun? I don't think so. I believe we did the right thing. Today, my daughters now own laptops and smart phones, as do I, along with hundreds of millions of others. "To everything, there is a season, and a time to every purpose, under heaven," wrote songwriter Pete Seeger, quoting the famous Bible verse.

We instituted a new rule at babysitting co-op. No electronic games. No cell phones. I've discussed our anti-electronics stance with dozens of parents over the years. At babysitting co-op, we allowed the kids to watch a video after supper before getting them ready for bed. Watching together was a group experience, and the parents controlled the on/ off switch. Would it have been better if, instead of watching videos, we had engaged in Saturday night imagination games with the kids and banned electronics altogether? Perhaps. But we chose a course of moderation. When I was in college, I sat in on a lecture delivered by a visiting East Indian guru, Swami Satchinanda, with a long gray beard and a saffron robe. He said, "Everything in moderation—a little of this, a little of that." I've always thought that made sense.

Our babysitting co-op lasted for twelve and a half years. But one Saturday night fifteen-year-old Nina's mom called and said, "I'm really sorry, but Nina can't come to co-op tonight. She's got a date with her boyfriend."

To paraphrase the poet Geoffrey Chaucer, all good things must come to an end. But I was saddened. A successful experiment in co-operative, cost-free childcare had come to an end. The amazing thing was these kids had become such good friends that they were well into ninth grade before they stopped coming to babysitting co-op. And they still see each other socially today.

My wife and I estimated that each family in our co-op saved over twenty thousand dollars in babysitting fees over those twelve and a half years. Plus, we initiated long-term friendships between both the parents and the kids. And we had engaged in a fruitful, ongoing dialogue together about child-rearing, including how to deal with the multi-screen media environment. We made rules, and we stuck with them. And we had a terrific time.

CHAPTER THIRTEEN

TV CARTOON SCANDALS— MEDIA AWARENESS FOR CHILDREN

Ms. Matsamura's Alessandro Elementary School classroom was packed with eight-year-old school children. They were excited. The regular schedule of classes had been interrupted for Allesandro School's annual Career Day. The hallways were crowded with professional athletes, actors, firemen, policemen, uniformed soldiers, doctors, engineers, some with gifts to give out to the children, some having driven their Los Angeles City emergency vehicles onto the large asphalt playground where children crowded around police cars, ambulances, and fire trucks that glistened in the sun.

My Career Day name tag said, *Voice of G.I. Joe's Flint and Radio & TV Announcer*. I was proud to be there. Student Council volunteers helped me with my boom box and my portfolio of illustrated cartoon boards. Long-time Allesandro School Principal, Lynn Andrews, greeted each of the Career Day volunteers. Thanks to Principal Andrews' ongoing efforts, Career Day at Allesandro was well organized and attracted dozens of professionals from all over Los Angeles. I was there to tell kids how I got into the business of film and television, how a student can take radio and TV production classes in high school and college, and how, if you enjoy talking in funny voices, you can study cartoon voice acting. But I also had a hidden agenda.

The first wave of Hasbro/G.I. Joe action figures and play sets based on characters from the cartoon had just hit store shelves. Hasbro was now spending tens of millions of dollars on TV advertising to get kids into stores to buy *G.I. Joe* toys. I felt I needed to do something to help level the playing field between this behemoth toy company and young consumers.

I had created a live program to take into schools entitled "TV Cartoon Scandals: Media Awareness for Children." It was my goal to focus kids' attention on the nature of commercials, electronic media, and the primary purpose of children's entertainment programming: to sell things to young consumers.

I edited together snippets of audio of my commercial voiceovers and bits from the *G.I. Joe* TV cartoon. I enlisted an artist friend, Jerry Liebowitz, to illustrate in cartoon style a half-dozen large foam-core poster boards with a few simple scenarios that would show, in pictures, how and why commercials are made. I printed up a simple flyer and dropped it off at Alessandro School and requested that it be distributed to LA Unified School District teachers and administrators. And soon my phone began to ring with calls from teachers and vice principals from dozens of schools inviting me to come to their classrooms. I asked the callers what prompted them to contact me.

They responded, "Our students are watching too much TV at home. It's getting in the way of doing their schoolwork. It's a big problem with our kids."

As I entered Ms. Matsamura's classroom, an EMT was finishing her Career Day presentation to the kids about what it was like to drive an ambulance and save people from accidents and illness. The kids were riveted. As I sat waiting for my turn to talk about my career in the media, I recalled the movie *City Slickers*, in which actor Billy Crystal tries to explain to his son's class on Career Day, "I sell air." (He was a radio advertising salesman. The kids were bored.) I hoped this wouldn't be my fate at Allesandro. Having performed for kids in the past, I tried to remember four things: be fast, loud, funny, and interactive. The EMT finished up her presentation to the kids. I removed the foam-core poster boards from my portfolio and set my boom box on Ms. Matsamura's desk.

"Hi, kids. I am a cartoon voice and a radio and TV announcer."

They stared blankly. I put my hand to my ear and spoke in my broadcast voice, "Today on Channel Seven Eyewitness News, it's Career Day at Allesandro School. And right now, the whole school is rising up off its foundation, and it's about to fly off into space."

The kids' eyes widened. "You sound like the guy on TV," one little boy said.

"I am that guy."

"Wow," they murmured.

"So, kids, what time of day do you get home from school?" I asked. "Raise your hands."

A few checked their watches, and a little girl shouted, "Three-thirty."

"Three-thirty. Good. Now, how often does this happen to you? You come home and everybody is watching TV. Their eyes are glued to the TV set, and one of them says to you, 'Shhh, be quiet, we're watching TV.'"

A little boy in the back row shouted, "Every day! That happens to me every day."

"And what are they watching on TV?" I asked. "They're watching a commercial . . . for diapers!"

The class laughed. I pressed play on my boom box. Cued up was my voiceover for an Ultra-Pampers-Plus TV commercial: "Introducing a diaper with the air-dry system, different because the top sheet has air pockets right underneath . . . "

"Different . . . ?" I asked the class. "It's a diaper. How can it be different?" (More laughter.)

"Let's say your mom is out shopping for diapers for the baby. Do you think if she brought home a box of Huggies the baby would be disappointed because they aren't Ultra-Pampers-Plus with the air-dry system?"

"N-O-O-O!" screamed the class.

"But isn't the Pampers commercial right? Aren't Pampers better than Huggies?"

"No," a few of them yelled. There were some looks of mild confusion.

A complex, critical dialogue with eight-year-olds about the nature and purpose of TV advertising had begun. I took out my first cartoon board—a drawing of an angry old man in a shoe store wearing a suit with his fists clenched and steam coming out of his nostrils. "Mr. Grump" stood in front of an empty cash register and a stack of unsold high-heeled jogging shoes for kids. A young person cowered before him.

"Now, this is Mr. Grump. He owns Grump's Shoe Store, and he's really mad at your cousin here, who works in Grump's Shoe Store to earn a few extra dollars to pay for his college textbooks. 'You haven't sold a single pair of my high-heeled jogging shoes all day. I'm going to have to fire you!' shouts Mr. Grump.

"'No, Mr. Grump, please don't fire me. I need the job,' says your cousin. 'If these high-heeled jogging shoes are made for kids, shouldn't you advertise them to kids?'

"'Advertise?!? I've already got a sign in the window,' says Mr. Grump. 'What do you mean, advertise to kids?'"

Mr. Grump's sign says, SALE—High-heeled jogging shoes, with a descending series of sale prices ending in the offer of spare change.

"So, kids," I asked, "What does your cousin mean when he says Mr. Grump should advertise to kids?"

The answers from the class included many of the ways sponsors advertise products to young consumers. I am always surprised at the level of sophistication young children have about the media. By grade-school age, they are already quite experienced. They've spent a lot of time online and in front of a TV set. Plus, when children offer their answers, it is a good opportunity to praise them for their ideas and participation.

"Mr. Grump should advertise on TV," volunteered a little girl in the front row.

"Yes, absolutely right. Mr. Grump should advertise on TV, so kids will see his commercial and get their moms to come in and buy the high-heeled jogging shoes. And where else can he advertise besides TV?"

"On the internet?" said a child in the back of the class.

"Yes, on the internet. There are thousands of commercials on the internet. Where else can Mr. Grump advertise his high-heeled jogging shoes? How about on those big signs on the freeway?"

"Billboards," said a little boy in the second row.

"Yes, billboards. You see them all over town advertising everything from cars to soft drinks to shoe stores. Where else . . . the radio?"

"Yeah, on the radio," shouted the kids.

"Any place else? How about those handbills they put on peo-ple's front doors, or the ads on the sides of busses?" Heads nodded enthusiastically.

"Okay, now, what TV shows do you guys watch?" The class shouted out a barrage of TV show titles.

"Now, I'm a grownup, and on TV when the commercials come on they try to sell me cars, clothes, life insurance, but what do they try to sell to kids . . . what do they try to sell to you?"

Ms. Matsamura's third-graders thought about this for a moment before they began to list what came to mind—toys, computers, candy, snack food, etc. I acknowledged each child's answer and continued to coax from them a growing list of products that are sold specifically to children.

"How about breakfast cereal? Have you ever been in the grocery store with your mom and you see a two-year-old sitting in the grocery cart with his plump little legs sticking out, and he's yelling, 'Mommy, I want *Teenage Mutant Ninja Turtles* cereal!' And everybody in the store is staring because this kid is not giving up, and finally, out of frustration, the mom grabs a box and hands it to him. Now that kid is hardly old enough to talk. How does he even know how to ask for *Teenage Mutant Ninja Turtles* cereal?"

A bright-looking little girl in the front row put up her hand. "He saw it on TV."

"Yes, he saw it on TV. Kids watch TV commercials. And they remember what they see on TV. And that's why Mr. Grump finally decides to advertise his high-heeled jogging shoes on TV. But he doesn't know anything about advertising. So he looks up advertising in the Yellow Pages—the big yellow soft-cover book filled with advertisements for everything you can think of. It's also a website—yellowpages.com. So Mr. Grump looks up advertising in The Yellow Pages under A, for advertising, and he sees an ad for Mr. Speedy's Advertising Company—*We Do Advertising Fast!* So he calls up Mr. Speedy."

On cartoon board #2, a now-smiling Mr. Grump has a light bulb over his head, and he is handing Mr. Speedy a wad of cash. On board #3 the popular Spanish-speaking radio personality, Humberto Luna, holds up a high-heeled jogging shoe and talks into a microphone.

"Humberto Luna, *el annunciador numero uno en el mundo*, will narrate Mr. Grump's commercial in Spanish, and maybe I can get the voiceover job in English! But wait a minute. What is Humberto Luna going to say in Mr. Grump's commercial? And what will I say in English? 'Mr. Grump's shoes are really . . . uh . . . dumb?'"

"N-O-O-O," moaned the kids.

"So what should the commercial say?"

The children furrowed their brows, then one little girl piped up, "Mr. Grump's shoes are really pretty."

"Yes. Excellent. 'Mr. Grump's shoes are really pretty.' That's exactly the kind of thing they say in a commercial. What else should we say about Mr. Grump's shoes?"

Hands went up. A chubby little boy in a striped t-shirt said, "Mr. Grump's high-heeled jogging shoes make you go really fast."

"Yes, there you go. 'Mr. Grump's high-heeled jogging shoes make you go really fast.'"

And on it went until the class had created an abundance of descriptive, colorful advertising slogans for Mr. Grump's shoe commercial. I repeated each line the kids authored and acknowledged each of them for their contributions.

One little girl suggested, "You should hire actors to hold the shoes." This is a very sophisticated idea from an eight-year-old child who appeared to have already peeled away a layer from the advertising onion. She sensed that the individuals selling things on television are hired to sell—that they aren't real people; they are actors. To them, what they see online and on television is unquestionably real and compelling. And that includes commercials aimed at children.

Cartoon board #4 shows Mr. Speedy racing from the recording studio to KBUX Radio & TV with a reel of recording tape under his arm.

"And with all your great ideas, kids, there goes Mr. Speedy across Sunset Boulevard to the studios of KBUX-Big Bucks Radio & TV to put Mr. Grump's commercial on the air. Inside KBUX, they're showing Mr. Grump's shoes on the morning show, and down the hall, famous radio DJ, Rick Dees, is on the air live, saying, 'Alright, everybody, we'll be right back after our first-ever Mr. Grump's High-Heeled Jogging Shoe commercial.'

"Mr. Grump's commercial plays on radio and TV all over town, and who should be watching? Why, it's your Mama!"

Cartoon board #5 shows a large woman with her hair in rollers, watching TV, and listening to the radio as Mr. Grump's commercial plays. The children groaned and giggled at the cartoon image of Mom in curlers. A large thought bubble appears above her head featuring the image of herself, Daddy, two kids, and the dog, all wearing Mr. Grump's high-heeled jogging shoes.

"And Mom thinks to herself, 'This commercial is amazing. It's taking over my brain. I am going to buy a pair of Mr. Grump's high-heeled jogging shoes for myself, for Daddy, Sissy, Sonny, and the doggy.'

"But Mom, that's going to be expensive," I warn. "A pair for everybody in the family and two for the dog! Kids, what's $39.95 times six? That's nearly $240."

At the end of the half-hour session, the eager kids in Miss Matsamura's class helped me pack up my cartoon story boards. By populating the story of advertising with a cast of characters—Mr. Grump, the young shoe store clerk, Mr. Speedy, Umberto Luna, and Rick Dees—and by encouraging kids to verbalize their thoughts about TV commercials—what they consist of, and what they sell—children begin to understand the players and can move toward demystifying the process of advertising, which is by nature a manipulation, a slight-of-hand, and for most viewers, especially children, a mystery.

CHAPTER FOURTEEN

WHAT THE SHRINK SAID

I attended a parents' meeting at a private grade school where a child psychologist was presenting his thoughts on children and digital media. It sounded promising. This school had a reputation for excellent academics and a humane, child-friendly atmosphere. The psychologist treated some of the students in the school as patients, so the administration felt safe in inviting him to speak on a topic everyone knew would be popular with parents.

The lecture hall filled up quickly. Parents were hoping to hear some answers about how digital technology affects their children, how much time spent in front of screens is too much, and how parents can regulate its usage. But what we got instead was a stern indictment of the internet as a haven for voyeurs and child predators. We've all heard discomfiting stories of underage kids running away for a secret tryst with someone they met on the internet. That is the kind of stories the psychologist told that night.

The first time I tried to warn my daughters about online predators in chatrooms, they rolled their eyes and informed me that they had been given extensive internet security training at school. Their computer teachers had instructed them not to give out personal information online, and they were told how to deal with suspicious strangers in a chat room, email, or list-serve. I heaved a tentative sigh of relief.

But according to the psychologist at the meeting I attended, the internet is a child molester's dream come true. I grew impatient. Yes, children need to be careful on the internet. But this man was telling us horror stories.

I raised my hand, "Sir, I have no doubt that what you're telling us is true. There are awful things that happen because of the internet. But I think the major concern is how to control the use of electronic media in the home with our kids."

Heads nodded. The psychologist heard me. He shifted gears and began to suggest that we search the internet for websites and organizations that offer advice to parents on tactics and strategies that can be used with children for controlling screen time.

Ironically, the best place to turn to for information about controlling the internet *is* the internet. The magic of the web is that you can Google just about anything and get thousands of suggestions and links instantly. You can search for key phrases like "children's media watchdog groups," "children's media education," "parenting strategies for internet use," "regulating children's TV and internet use," etc. Try your own phrases. The possibilities are nearly endless, and the resources on the web for parents are abundant. If you want to look for help locally, simply add the name of the town where you live to your search phrase, and you'll find something (e.g., "parent media watchdog groups Salt Lake City").

Here are some useful places to start:

- Common Sense Media (www.CommonSenseMedia.org)
- National Institute on Media and the Family (www.ParentFurther.com)

- The American Academy of Pediatrics (www.Pediatrics.aap-publications.org)
- U.S. Department of Justice (www.OJJDP.gov/publications/ncjrslibrary.html)
- A media activist mom who is interesting to check out is Janell Burley Hoffman (www.JanellBurleyHofmann.com)
- An organization of educators is Teachers Resisting Unhealthy Children's Entertainment—TRUCE (www.TRUCETeachers.org)
- One of many effective parent organizations is Media! Tech! Parenting! (www.MediaTechParenting.net)

The above list is just a tiny fraction of the thousands of helpful websites and resources available to parents on the issue of media and children. Another good place to look is close to home—your neighbors, your children's school, your babysitting group, your local school board, and your place of worship. The concerns you have about your children and the media are shared by almost everyone, even your children. They know when they're spending too much time gaming or online or in front of the TV set. They can feel it. They just might not know how to stop. That's where you come in.

My most precious memories of my children's early years are of conversations we had together—in the car, at the breakfast table, before bedtime. And this is where discussions about screen time can be had. Parents have varying childrearing agendas and many areas of human behavior we want to discuss with our children. And it's all too easy to let opportunities slip by. With difficult subjects that might lead to conflict, it's often easier to say nothing and just pray that our kids will do the right thing. But conversations with young children are easier to have than you might think.

Most kids are eager to engage with their parents, express their opinions, and explore their developing thinking. This can lead families to fruitful, constructive conversations about watching TV, using smart phones, web surfing, gaming, etc. Do you need to have a firm position formulated before you speak with your kids? Not necessarily. Every child is different. And what you say to your child when dealing with questions, opinions, and educated guesses may differ from child to child. The important thing is to have the dialogue. We're dealing with questions, opinions, and educated guesses. The long-term effects of excessive internet use on children are unknown. Only preliminary studies have been done. But we do know that too much screen time, regardless of which kind of screen, is the same as watching too much TV. At best, it's a time-waster.

CHAPTER FIFTEEN

MOTH

:mains happy and sane in this over- in one of the most undigital activities g. For years, my wife's parents, Jack stay at our house during the Christ- threw a New Year's Eve party in their ...., - g-- ---red with the same cheap champagne and bacon-wrapped weenie hors d'oeuvres, so I changed the rules. I asked our guests, young and old, to prepare an act of some sort—a joke, a poem, a family reminiscence, a song, or a story. My wife begged me not to bar the door to anyone who refused to sing for their supper. I didn't have to.

To my surprise most of our invitees heartily agreed to my terms. Some brought jokes, a few read poems, some sang songs, and many told stories. Our homegrown New Year's Eve cabaret turned out to be a joyous celebration, not only of our friends' singing voices and their ability to rhyme, but also of the deep and affecting charm of their varied personalities and stories. We asked everyone to turn off their mobile phones, and, after the requisite snacks and libations, we sat back and enjoyed each other's songs and stories.

The best storyteller of the evening was Grandpa Jack Corwin, who, at age eighty-three, had begun taking a senior memoir writing class at his local adult school. The stories he read for us that night of growing up poor during the Great Depression were fascinating.

Ours was not the only party to implement this entertaining tradition. One evening in New York City in 1997, Georgia-born novelist George Dawes Green invited friends over to his New York apartment and asked them to tell five-minute personal stories. The evening was so successful that his friends urged him to make the storytelling a regular event.

Green formed an organization called The Moth (TheMoth.org), dedicated to the art of personal storytelling. The name is derived from Green's childhood memories of friends and family telling stories at night out on the porch as moths flitted against the screen. The Moth, a non-profit organization, curates travelling stage shows and sponsors storytelling contests in coffee houses, theaters, and night clubs around the country. *The Moth Radio Hour* recently won The Peabody Award, an honor granted to radio and TV shows for quality storytelling. The Peabody judges said, "Storytelling, likely the oldest art, is revered and reinvigorated by this hour for everyday raconteurs."

Every week on the radio, you can listen to storytelling programs like *This American Life, Snap Judgment,* and *The Moth Radio Hour.* Local storytelling guilds around the country produce their own radio programming and podcasts. I'm not advocating that everyone must do what The Moth's George Dawes Green did; but an organized evening of storytelling with friends and family or a night out at a local storytelling show is eminently doable, and there's a lot of room for fun.

On the third Tuesday of every month, Club Los Globos on Sunset Boulevard in East Hollywood hosts a Moth Story Slam. Every month, I check The Moth's website for the evening's theme. Recently, the theme was "Escape." My wife and I fixed a quick supper, then drove to Los Globos. I rehearsed my story in the car. As always, before telling a personal story to a live audience, I was a bit nervous. The story I would tell that night was about me and my friend Gerry O'Reilly and the fateful summer morning when we barely escaped from some girls' apartment, chased out by one very angry mom.

My wife and I stood on the sidewalk in line outside Club Los Globos. When we reached the door, we paid our eight dollars admission and started up the wooden staircase leading to the ballroom, which was already full of people who had come to hear the story slam. At the apron of the stage, storytellers filled out release forms and tossed them into a tote bag, which is used to determine who will tell the first story of the night. A tall thirty-something host mounted the stage, welcomed the crowd, and explained the rules.

"The Moth is about true stories," he said. "We don't have fact checkers, but we have volunteer judges, and we want to hear five-minute stories that have a beginning, middle, and end, stories that have some stakes, and that hold our interest. The winner of tonight's story slam will go on to compete in The Moth Grand Slam, and the Grand Slam winner will fly to New York for The Annual Moth Ball."

I tossed my release form into the bag with thirty or so others. Names would be randomly drawn throughout the evening, and ten of us would be called on stage to tell a five-minute personal story during the two-hour program. Storytelling at The Moth isn't just the opening act for a larger evening of entertainment. It is the main event. This young standing-room-only crowd of around two hundred was there to listen to stories.

There were a few gray-haired folks like myself in the audience, but most were in their late twenties and early thirties—the digital generation who spend their days working on computers, web-surfing, texting, and checking their Instagram, Snapchat, and Facebook. But they come to The Moth for something different. A Moth Story Slam is about as far away as you can get from the wired world. Audiences come to witness their peers engage in an activity that has taken place at human gatherings since time immemorial—storytelling. For members of the digital generation, The Moth serves as an antidote to the high-tech realm they inhabit during the day. Except for the microphone and hi-tech stage lights, nothing marked this evening as anything other than a timeless human tradition.

That night, the stories ranged from humorous to tragic, embarrassing to mundane. After the fourth storyteller finished and the judges gave their scores, the host reached into the hat and pulled out my name. I took the long walk up the aisle to the stage. I was nervous as I always am before appearing in front of strangers. Would I forget my story and stare blankly into the stage lights? As I began to tell my intrepid tale, waves of welcome laughter erupted from the crowd. I made it through the story without stumbling, and the applause felt good. The judges awarded me generous scores.

Throughout the rest of the evening's stories, I kept an eye on the judges' tally board, and after the final storyteller, the host added up the scores and announced me as the winner of the story slam. I was ecstatic. I had participated in a time-honored ritual of telling tales before a crowd. For a couple of hours, a group of strangers shared foibles and missteps, both happy and sad. Our stories had brought us closer together.

Not long after the story slam, I received an email from the Moth-SHOP Community Education Program inviting me to attend a youth storytelling show at The Colburn School in downtown Los Angeles, next to the Museum of Contemporary Art. The MothSHOP conducts workshops with students and marginalized adults in underserved neighborhoods. The goal of the program is to enhance students' social, analytical, and literacy skills and improve academic performance and self-esteem.

The evening was sponsored by Participant Media, a Hollywood entertainment company. The Moth/Participant Media Summer Storytelling Series focused on the theme of "Standing Up." Through the workshops, students crafted stories of standing up to difficult circumstances and challenges. The public showcase featured school children telling stories they developed during the workshop.

It was an amazing evening. There were eight thirteen-year-olds on stage. One by one each of them stood up and delivered triumphant, often heart-rending stories of overcoming adversity and standing up for themselves. Reporter James Rainey, who attended the show that night, wrote "The Colburn crowd cheered with abandon, some rising out of their seats."[32]

I feel a bit like an evangelist when I write about storytelling. I believe in the power of storytelling to heal us in this digital, impersonal age. Judging by the number of live storytelling shows in theaters around town these days, I'm happy to say that storytelling has become nearly as popular as standup comedy. Storytelling is not everyone's cup of tea, but the fact that we have a place to go where we can listen to fellow humans transport us to another world with a simple story can be a great relief from our wired, work-a-day world. Storytelling events offer families an antidote to the techno-stress and cold-bloodedness that sometimes characterizes contemporary digital life.

Confronting the obstacles for families in our digital age can either be a battle or a creative challenge. I find that with a little improvisation, creativity, and the desire to try new things like storytelling, we can lighten our load and inject fun into our lives in simple ways.

CHAPTER SIXTEEN

FAMILIES TALK

The media is full of prescriptions for how families can handle digital technology and electronic entertainment in the home; however, each family has unique needs and values, and each family must determine the principles and practices that will work for them. I interviewed a number of families—both parents and children—to see how they do it. The opinions expressed are solely those of the people I interviewed, but there is so much we can learn from the opinions of others.

The following are transcriptions of live interviews I conducted with real people from a variety of backgrounds—school teachers, a psychologist, a website designer, a new media consultant, an electrical contractor, and their children. I interviewed the children separately, followed by their parents, and I asked each person to recall their memories of how and why TV, videos, cell phones, computers, game platforms, and other digital devices were regulated and controlled in their home. I asked what the rules were and whether or not the rules actually worked. And I asked if regulating technology in the home affected the academic success of their children. I also asked the same questions of my own children.

Sort through these suggestions and examples, and decide which practices will be most helpful to your family.

FAMILY #1: LARRY, ANNA MARIE, NINA, AND MARC

Larry is a psychologist. His wife, Anna Marie, teaches college courses in New Media. Their two children, Nina, and her younger brother, Marc, are both college students.

THE PARENTS

Q: How was technology used in your house when the kids were little?

Anna Marie: When my daughter, Nina, was two years old, she was using my Macintosh computer drawing pictures with Kid Pix software. She sat in the den with her little legs dangling off the stool, and she'd call me, "Mommy, I need a new background color."

For our family, it wasn't about restricting access to a computer; it was about educating our kids about what a computer is for, what it's capable of. In order to survive in the workplace, our kids were going to have to be computer literate. Why not teach them early? If I had it to do over again, I'd reward my kids with free computer time in exchange for their taking computer programming classes. As it was, we allowed them TV and gaming time when they finished their homework. It worked out. They're both in college, doing well.

Q: Did problems arise in your home around the kids' use of technology?

Larry: As a little girl, Nina watched videos over and over again, so the issue developed: was the VCR a time-suck? Of course it was. So we imposed a loose set of rules about homework having to be done before the kids could watch videos. They were busy with after-school athletics and music lessons, and they weren't latch-key kids, so there wasn't much time to watch TV or videos. I do remember we had an issue with AOL Instant Messaging, which was very popular for a while. We talked with Nina about how she should respond if she were ever confronted with chats that made her uncomfortable, and this seemed to make things easier for all of us to deal with. We were lucky. Nina was always a good student; she chose friends we liked. When she got to high school, there of course was a bit of separation, which is quite normal, and we didn't know all of her friends, but I never felt I had to engage in any type of surveillance or spying on her. She was a trustworthy kid. She led a fairly transparent life, didn't hide much from us. And we respected her privacy.

Q: Did your children have free access to computers?

Anna Marie: By the time our kids turned eleven, they each had their own computer. In our house, I was the person who did the computer setup and maintenance, so my kids knew I was available to them to deal with almost any issue that came up with the computers in our house without snooping in any way. I'll never forget my nine-year-old son pointing out some pornographic search results that came up on Google. He was shocked. So we talked about it. I'm not sure how you avoid it these days, but it never became a problem. We were candid about it and not punitive.

Q: Was there a difference between the way your son and your daughter used technology?

Larry: When Nintendo came out with its first gaming platform, Marc took to it right away, so we had to impose time limits on gaming. And we were concerned about content. Marc played mainly sports-related games. There are games available to these kids where they can steal cars, beat prostitutes, and kill people. Add to that the repetitious nature of gaming and the dulling of kids' sensibilities concerning sex and violence, and you have a recipe for disaster. That troubled me greatly. We felt that games like *Grand Theft Auto* were wholly inappropriate for a twelve-year-old boy, so we talked with Marc about why we didn't like games with violent and sexual content, and we simply didn't allow those games in our house. We kept Marc busy with sports and music, so there wasn't a lot of time for gaming.

Q: In hindsight, would you have handled technology differently?

Anna Marie: Knowing what I know now, I would have tied our restrictions to learning more about the inner workings of the computer. I would have pushed my kids more to learn about the underlying mechanism. It's easier these days. They offer computer coding courses for elementary school kids now. Parents can sign kids up for online computer learning courses in game design. They're finding that some kids learn better through interactive learning applications. That's the kind of thing that kids need to be doing rather than just sitting passively twisting a joy stick and watching things blow up on a screen.

Q: Were there conflicts in your family over the use of technology?

Larry: It wasn't all carefree discussion. We definitely had conflicts, especially with our son, about how much time he wanted to spend with his computer games. Gaming was definitely his go-to activity. We never imposed an outright ban, but neither of us were comfortable with allowing him to play his computer games all afternoon. My position was, "Okay, that's enough, let's do something else." We had an intuitive sense that gaming was addictive, and it was our responsibility to moderate the use of it. His older sister was an avid reader. She walked around with a book under her arm, but we had to push Marc to read. And by his senior year in high school, he did develop an interest in extracurricular reading. So if I had it to do all over again, I would have done the same thing. I wouldn't have been tougher or harder on my son; I just would have kept the same discussion going, expressing my opinion—shaming a kid for their behavior is not only ineffective but can also be destructive of the relationship between a parent and a child.

Q: If you had to give younger families advice about technology, what would you tell them?

Anna Marie: Tomorrow's digital parents will have increasingly difficult problems, not only because of the number of screens and delivery systems, but also because of the big internet carriers like Comcast, AT&T, and Verizon, which are monetizing what used to be free and slowing down the delivery of services like YouTube. There will be a big digital divide between those who can afford to buy tiered internet access and those who can't. The golden age of net neutrality and free web access to knowledge and information is going away as we witness the concentration of corporate power. Plus, the next generation of digital parents faces huge security and privacy issues as the web gets better at tracking and sucking up all our private data. The next time your child signs up on a social media network, you might want to read the terms of service agreement and find out what rights you're actually giving up before you click "I Agree."

Larry: The technology may change, but family relationships are a constant. Parents and children need to negotiate the technology together. The situation you have to negotiate may change—whether it's a cell phone, a game, a curfew, an automobile, an illegal substance, or a bad friend—but the skillset a parent must call upon to set a limit and enforce it remains the same.

Regarding parental controls, Larry also reported that there are some parents who feel so strongly about shielding their children from violence that they try and prevent their kids from even imagining that they are playing with a gun. Larry pointed out that it is normal for children to exhibit aggressive behavior while playing with one another—setting up scenarios in which there are good guys and bad guys or rivalries where children attempt to dominate and vanquish each other, often with toy or make-believe weapons. To draw a connection between this kind of play and the use of real weapons to inflict actual violence is something different altogether. Children engage in spontaneous play-acting in which the aggressive impulse and violence are expressed through pretend play. It might be imitative and based on what they see in TV shows, movies, or computer games, but it is an active form of imagination play which is initiated by the players and resolved one way or another through the storyline they create together.

However, with today's violent, high-budget computer games, the viewer is neither initiating nor imagining but rather is sitting passively, watching a violent scenario written and produced for the purpose of entertaining the viewer with a complex and skillfully assembled series of violent images and giving him the illusion of firing a weapon or stealing a fast car.

The production budget for the computer game *Grand Theft Auto: Five* (GTA5) was 265 million dollars. *Hollywood Reporter* magazine reported that within three days of its release to the public, GTA5 had earned over a billion dollars. The user of a highly sophisticated interactive media game is essentially a watcher, a titillated button-pusher. Mental health professionals and educators believe that the repetitive and demonstrably addictive nature of computer gaming, if consisting of violent and sexual imagery, can desensitize the player to the effects of violence and violently sexual acts, reducing the natural level of empathy in a child. This is why responsible parents intuitively feel they should restrict their kids' access to these kinds of games.

THE KIDS

Q: How did you use new technology when you were a kid?

Marc: When I was seven, I really wanted a Gameboy. The color unit was just coming out. My parents made a deal with me. I had to finish my first book, and it had to be at least one hundred pages long. I read a book, and they got me a Gameboy. But there were rules. My mom would definitely get on my case if I played too much, and if I did, she'd say, "Okay, no Gameboy for a week." Once she threatened to sell my game console. She did take it away a few times, but she didn't sell it. Then I got an Xbox for Christmas, and I got good at looking out the window and checking to see if my parents were coming up the driveway, because I knew they would get mad at me for playing more than I was supposed to.

Q: What kinds of rules were set about electronic media in your house?

Nina: Our parents weren't that strict, really. There weren't parental controls on the TV or our computers. But they were concerned with content. If we wanted to watch *South Park*, we had to go to a friend's house. If I were a babysitter and I had to set rules for kids, I definitely wouldn't let them sit all day gaming or watching videos. This is why I don't like babysitting. Kids take advantage of you. "Oh, our mom lets us watch." But you have different instructions from the parents, but you don't want to come off as a bad person, but, hey, they're not your kids.

Q: Do you remember how your parents tried to enforce the rules regarding technology?

Marc: Both my parents worked and got home around supper time. My sister and I got home from school earlier, and we'd tell the babysitter, "Look, it's okay with my parents that I use my Gameboy. I've done my homework." And when I got home from school, whether I was with friends or not, the first thing I'd do was turn on my Gameboy. But my parents checked our homework every day, so I couldn't play games 24/7. And I played mainly sports games. They didn't allow stuff like *Grand Theft Auto*. They didn't want us watching sex and violence. When I wanted a new game, my dad would take me to the game store so he knew what I was getting. But at a certain point in high school, I lost interest in gaming. There wasn't much storyline or plot to them. I took an Advanced Placement

Literature course, and I realized I liked reading and that I spent too much time gaming, so I sold my Xbox and bought a ticket for a rock festival.

Q: Both you kids are in college. Do you think access to all this technology has affected your ability as students?

Nina: If my brother had told me in high school that he was going to be a math major in college, I wouldn't have believed him. He and I watched a lot of TV together. But he's doing great.

And college has its own unique challenges. College teachers are cracking down these days. A lot of my professors don't allow laptops in class because they know kids are on Facebook, Instagram, and Pinterest, and they aren't listening to the lecture. I'm a Teaching Assistant in graduate school, and I see kids working on papers or online shopping when they're supposed to be paying attention to Statistics. So at least half the professors in my college have banned electronics from the classroom. Kids can't seem to help themselves and can't stay off social media, while their parents have shelled out hundreds of thousands of dollars for college tuition.

I have to admit that when I'm doing homework outside of class, I have my email open; I have iChat on my computer so I can text my friends. I'll jump around from working on my thesis to doing analysis for something else; an email will come in, and I'll answer it immediately because I see it pop up on my screen. So I rarely start and complete a single task in one sitting these days. I'm always multitasking, and I'm definitely less focused because of it. I'm not sure that all this technology is much of a help when it's all turned on at the same time.

My mom was an early adopter of technology, so my brother and I grew up with computers and games and art software. I think that was an advantage. Being technologically savvy in today's world is crucial. I have wonderful memories of being in the editing room with my mom at work when I was little. She had a 1990s version of

The Sims on her computer, and she'd let me create cities and natural disasters, and it was all in black and white—super old school. But I don't play computer games anymore.

Mark: If I could go back in time and change how I did things as a kid, I probably would have read more. I probably would have done more math, practiced it more. Just to get used to it, because it would do wonders in the future. I definitely wish I would have spent less time playing video games and more time reading. I think I would be more developed now. I'm fine, but I think I could be better.

Marc no longer plays computer games. He is in his third year of college majoring in Mathematics.

His older sister, Nina, is in graduate school majoring in International Studies. Nina recently landed a job in a Washington, DC, social science research firm.

FAMILY #2: SARA

Sara is a married mother of three children, ages twelve, eighteen, and twenty. She is the oldest of ten children born into a middle-class midwestern family. Sara designs websites and print graphics.

Q: When was the first time you felt there was an issue with your kids and electronic media?

Sara: Before I became a parent, I actually developed somewhat of a plan with my husband. We believed that our job as parents was to raise kids to become self-confident people, who by the age of eighteen would be able to leave home and become viable adults. Our plan as parents involved a way to deal with technology in the home. By the time my husband and I got together, I had seen so much digital chaos in other people's homes that I knew we had to get a handle on technology for our kids. And this wasn't just about forbidding kids from using technology. It was about learning how to use a computer responsibly for things like online banking, homework, and keeping up with world news.

We live in a digital world, and so much of education and commerce is computer based that we figured it was important for our kids to learn about technology and how to use it responsibly and in moderation. If you don't know how to use technology today, you can't be a viable adult, and you probably won't have marketable skills. It's not just about how to use technology but also when and why to use it. I think the modern parent has to do a lot more than just show up at your kid's sixth birthday party with a box full of digital technology and say, "Woohoo, isn't this fun and pretty and wonderful?"

I was the oldest of ten children in a religious family where my parents didn't allow television, computers, or electronic media of any kind. I assume this was because of teachings in their church, but my parents never gave a reason why we didn't have TV, videos, or computers in our house. When we asked why, we were told, "Because we said so."

I became a voracious reader. I spent a lot of time at the library, and I'm thankful to my parents for that. But when we visited a friend's house, we binged on television. I couldn't understand how a friend was able to watch a favorite program on TV and then just turn it off and walk away. I wanted to watch on and on, probably because I was deprived of TV and videos in my house. And there was no discussion about it in our home. We simply weren't allowed any electronic media.

So I've done the opposite, really. My husband and I have a very active and conscious dialogue with our kids about technology. We have certainly put controls on many things, but not as punishment, and the fact that we encourage discussion and negotiation with our kids has made it much easier on all of us. We know that modern education relies on iPads and computers, and I feel it's my responsibility to educate myself on what's out there, so I can teach my kids about social media, smart TVs, and web surfing, rather than be unpleasantly surprised by what I discover them doing on their own.

My siblings and I are raising kids now, and we are all over the map regarding technology. Some of us have no rules whatsoever, and some of us do it the old-fashioned way and have put a complete prohibition on modern media in the home. My mom still has underage kids in her house, and she just purchased their first computer in 2011. I have noticed that a number of my siblings became media addicts. As kids, we couldn't walk past the TV display in Best Buy without stopping and watching endlessly until someone dragged us away. The good news was some of us became voracious readers because, in our home, there wasn't much else to do. My library card was extremely well used.

I didn't like the fact that there was no discussion about media with my parents. So I decided what kind of parent I was going be around media way before I ever had kids. I was very clear that there was going to be discussion and dialogue in my home with my kids. And I was lucky enough to meet a man who was willing to talk about TV, computers, cellphones, social media—all of it. And that has done wonders for our kids.

Kids need to know what resources are out there for them. If a child isn't computer savvy, the chances of future employment are very limited. And at the same time, if they're allowed to do nothing but watch TV, web surf, and play video games, they'll grow up as couch potatoes. I'm horrified by some of the behavior of my kids' friends who can't even make eye contact with adults because they're always texting. That's hard to be around. It's like fingernails on a chalkboard. When I'm talking with someone, I want to talk with them, not watch them text someone else. Where's the new digital Emily Post when we need her?

Q: What do you do about computers in your home?

Sara: In our house, each of us has our own computer, but they're all in one central location. We converted our guest room into the computer room. That's where our kids can go online, do their homework, check their Facebook, whatever. But there is no technology in their bedrooms—no TV, no computer. A bedroom is a private place, and we want to keep the digital world out of our kids' bedrooms. They don't feel deprived; they have access to technology, but not all the time and not everywhere in the house. And if they want to take a cell phone call in their bedrooms, they can do that. We haven't taken away their privacy.

Homework is always done either at the dining room table or in the computer room. Homework is a family event. We do homework with our kids every day when they come home from school. I know a lot of families can't do that, but my husband and I both work out of our home, so we have that luxury of being there when our kids come home from school.

At one point, we had two TVs in the house, but we noticed that our kids would go off and veg out in front of the TV, so we sold one and kept one, and now, if our kids want to watch, they do it together. When we find them hanging out together, eating popcorn, watching a movie together, that's fine. TV and video watching is often a group activity in our house.

When each of our kids turned thirteen, we allowed them to ride the city bus, and we gave them each mobile phones, but not smart phones. There are just too many temptations on smart phones. Too many games and apps. And they can go online at school and at home.

They got all excited about texting, but we purposely avoided purchasing the texting option from our cell phone provider. We challenged our kids, "If you can give us a really good, logical reason that you need texting, we'll get it for you." And they couldn't. Oh, they say things like, "All our friends text," and I respond, "Yeah, but that's not a logical reason for you to text." So when they're in class or out with their friends, they don't have their faces buried in their cell phones texting all the time. We allow them to use Whatsapp so they can text if they have wifi access, so we're not anti-texting Luddites. We just want to keep it down to a dull roar.

We design technology use in our house so that when you're in a conversation with someone, you're not doing something else. And we ban cell phones from the dinner table. That's been a rule in our house from the beginning. And my husband and I have to serve as role models. We try to give our kids our full attention. And we always have dinner together. We have a phone-charging station in the kitchen, and when we're at home, our phones are there. If an important call comes through, we take it. Otherwise, the phones stay there. The cell phone doesn't follow you around. You go to the phone.

We didn't set this up as a hard-and-fast rule. We allowed pieces of technology into the kids' lives one by one when needed, rather than having it available all at once, slapping unenforceable rules on them. We started our kids out with a simple flip phone saying, "Here's a phone you can use to stay safe when you ride the bus to and from school." And then we'd get it back from them when they got home. And slowly they'd get to have it for longer periods of time. But they'd have to earn it by turning the phone on and off when appropriate, by taking our calls, and by calling to let us know where they were. We told our kids, "We're paying for this phone; don't take it for granted that you deserve a phone for no reason."

Facebook's rule is you can't have a page until you're thirteen, so we honored that rule. And we imposed it for other social media sites like Instagram, Snapchat, WeChat, etc. When the kids turned thirteen, we helped them set up their Facebook pages and imposed the rule that we had to be their Facebook friend; otherwise, no Facebook page.

The hard part of it is, as a parent, I feel I have to be up on all this technology. It's hard because it's changing all the time, but I feel it's my responsibility. How can I teach my kids something I don't know? We put a lot of thought into all this, and along the way, we improvised and changed strategies. Technology changes overnight—new social media sites, new devices—but we never forgot that it was our responsibility to have technology serve our needs and not enslave us and waste our time.

My sister became a step-parent and felt she had to establish her authority. She spends a lot of time taking her son's cell phone away from him, making it a punishment. She takes the TV and video remotes and locks them in her bedroom until she gets home every night. I think that's a little extreme, but it works for her.

My husband and I spend less time making technology a punitive thing. With us, it's more about rewarding good behavior. I think that the families that talk together about technology are the families that impress me the most. The little details and strategies we use are less important than an open, honest dialogue between parents and kids. That way it becomes more about sharing ideas than disciplining and banning things.

In our family, every step we take with technology comes with conversation between all of us. We try to demystify technology. These are tools and entertainment, and they all have their place. And we try to explain to our kids why we feel the way we do about all of it. We don't have terrible arguments with our teenagers, because we talk as a family. We don't just impose rules from on high. And we don't know it all. My daughter had to show me how Instagram works and why it's so cool. So sometimes the kids are the ones who are keeping us informed. And because we have an ongoing dialogue with them, they're forthcoming with what they know, they're not off in a corner plotting secret nefarious online activities. They come to us, and they are proud to share what they know.

If you teach a child how to learn and how to take in knowledge, I think they can get it from anywhere. It's about opening your mind and taking in information instead of sitting there and just being entertained. Opening a book or watching a documentary on Disovery.com—either one of those activities will give you knowledge if you allow yourself to be a conduit. You just have to teach a young mind how to do that, and I don't know if it matters whether you're getting it from a book or an iPad. What counts is training kids to soak up knowledge. We don't want the knowledge to go away.

FAMILY #3: BRIDGET, PETER, SONJA, AND STEFAN

Peter and Bridget were among the founding families of our babysitting co-op. Peter grew up in Germany and works as an electrical contractor and solar energy systems designer. Bridget grew up in Jamaica and is a public school teacher who specializes in teaching hearing-impaired children. They both immigrated to America when they were in their twenties. They met in the United States, got married, and had two children together. Their daughter, Sonja, is four years older than her brother, Stefan. Both children are now college students.

THE PARENTS

Q: Did you make rules about watching TV, videos, or new media in your home when the kids were little?

Bridget: Our older child, Sonja, never really liked watching TV. She was a social child, and she preferred to hang out or play with her toys rather than watch TV. Our neighbor had the Baby Songs videos: "My mommy comes back, she always comes back, she never will forget me." I actually tried to get Sonja to watch those, but she wasn't that interested.

In terms of rules for TV, homework had to be done first, and they could watch TV on the weekend, but there were certain things I wouldn't let them watch. *Power Rangers* was a big deal at the time, neighborhood kids wore Power Rangers costumes for Halloween. On the show, the characters blasted each other with ray guns and beat each other up with kung-fu, and I just didn't want my little boy imitating that kind of thing, so we didn't watch *Power Rangers*. And he wanted to watch *South Park*, but I felt that, as a little boy, he would imitate the bad language and the cynical meanness that is part of that show. It was a purely gut reaction. It wasn't based on anything more than "I just don't want you watching that nonsense."

Peter: We hardly watched any TV. And I didn't make any rules. If there were any rules, it was my wife who imposed them on the kids.

Q: What did you allow your kids to watch?

Bridget: They watched Disney videos; those videos were a staple of the babysitting co-op. When all the children came over on Saturday nights, the kids would play, we'd have supper together, and then we'd sit them down in front of the television set with a video to keep them busy for an hour and a half.

Q: Did you try to keep your kids from becoming avid TV watchers?

Bridget: TV was never a big deal in this house. I think it's a waste of time. We don't watch TV during the day. We're not big TV people. My son, Stefan, played in a rock band in high school, so he wasn't too interested in being a couch potato by that point.

We never allowed TV in their bedrooms. When they were little I didn't want my kids to be off in a room looking at something without my knowledge of what they were watching. I talk with parents at my school whose children have their own televisions in their rooms, and I never thought that was a good idea because you never know what they're watching or how much they're watching. TV becomes like a substitute family for some kids. Instead of sitting with your parents and watching TV and having conversations about what you're watching, you're by yourself in your room, and the family starts to grow apart. This was just a gut feeling of mine.

I have colleagues working in the schools who think that the amount of TV that children watch affects the way their brains develop. They should be outside playing, creating games, and getting a little dirty. I would rather have my kids down the street on their bicycles playing with friends, getting mud on their pants rather than having them sit in front of a TV set. That's just a notion that I have of raising kids—that TV and the internet are not family, they're not parents. I didn't want electronic media to be a babysitter for the kids. The kids would say, "We're bored. We're watching TV because we're bored." I'd say. "Turn the TV off. Go read a book. Only idiots are bored. There's lots to do in the world." I grew up in Jamaica, and I had to ask my parents' permission to watch TV. And that was only after I showed my parents that my homework was finished. I was raised in a strict, rather unyielding family. I just didn't think that my kids' lives should be about TV.

Peter: I grew up in Germany. We had three TV channels, so there wasn't that much for kids to watch, and except for the summer months, it was dark after supper, and that's when we were put to bed. And my parents would stay up reading.

Q: Did you have discussions with your kids about their use of digital technology in your home?

Bridget: It was important to me that I had conversations with my kids. And I had them do their homework close by—usually in the dining room. In high school, Stefan went to a neighborhood film school for kids, and they created videos, they learned to edit videos, and they cast each other in their productions. It was very creative. He took control of the medium rather than just watching it. These days Stefan comes home from college and watches movies, the Independent Film Channel, and Netflix. He's studying film theory and visual rhetoric at college, so I suppose he's doing more than just watching TV. He's analyzing TV in the context of his college courses, and I suppose that's better than being a couch potato. When I talk to him about all this, he's very articulate and clear. His professors have really sharpened his intellect in terms of politics and art and how media delivers messages to viewers. I'd like to think this is because we never really let him watch much frivolous stuff. His sister, Sonja, was on the track team in high school and ran cross-country, so she was either outdoors running or doing homework. She had AOL Instant Messenger on her computer upstairs in her room, but we didn't impose any rules on that.

Peter: The kids had to share a computer, and Stefan's older sister dominated it a bit, especially when instant messaging was popular. We purposely didn't get them their own laptops until they were in high school. And they never had a TV upstairs. When they wanted to watch TV, they had to come down to the living room.

Q: Did your kids play video games?

Bridget: When Stefan was in middle school, he played video games. We didn't buy the extra-ultra-violent-kill-people games.

Q: Did he ask for violent titles?

Bridget: Yes, but we said no. We didn't allow him to have them. There's too much violence in those games. He may have played them at friends' houses, but we didn't buy them for him. If a game was rated Mature, we didn't allow it. We adhered to the ratings system for video games. I felt that watching violent video games or TV shows would affect his thought processes somehow. I was like a police mom.

Q: Were there ever issues between you and the kids with cell phones?

Bridget: We got our kids Blackberries when they got to high school. What irritated me was when we would go out to eat as a family our son would bring his Blackberry along, and he wouldn't be a part of the conversation at supper, but that was near the end of high school when he was a typical teenage pain in the neck.

Q: Did you monitor your kids' use of the computer?

Bridget: Our kids never gave us reason not to trust them. We didn't monitor the histories on their web browsers. I do remember Stefan using my computer one day, and afterwards I got curious about where he had been browsing, and I found some sites on my computer that I'm sure he didn't want me to know about. I made a stink about it, and after that, he was more careful.

Q: Did social media ever cause problems for your kids?

Bridget: When our son was in high school, he saw an invitation to a party from a friend on Facebook, and he went to the party, and at two o'clock in the morning, we got a phone call: "Mom, I'm at the party, and there are lots of people here, and there are gunshots going off." We had to go and pick him up. That was a little scary. Fortunately, that wasn't a regular occurrence.

Q: In your work with children and education, have you seen things that shaped your philosophy about kids and electronic media?

Bridget: I make home-visits as part of my job, and in houses as small as our living room there will be TV's as big as the fireplace, and everyone will be watching. Not much else will be going on—no books, no conversation, just TV. And that's a strong image in my mind of the wrong way to go.

Peter: All the way through school, we kept an eye on their behavior, how they acted at home, how they did at school, and we didn't really see the need for much more than common sense restrictions.

They were good kids. They earned our trust. They're turning out pretty well.

THE KIDS

Q: What do you remember about your parents' attempts to control technology in your house when you were kids?

Sonja: As a little girl, I had to ask permission to watch TV. We were pretty restricted in what we could watch. I do remember sneaking and watching whatever I wanted on TV on the weekend when my parents went out on a date together. Before AOL Instant Messenger and texting, I remember being on the phone a lot with friends. But I was only allowed to do this when I finished my homework. My mom checked my homework, but in high school she trusted me. I was a hard worker, and I didn't need monitoring.

Stefan: My mom set guidelines for watching TV. She is a schoolteacher, so she sees first-hand the effects on her students of watching too much TV. Plus, she was turned off by the violence and bad taste on kids' TV. My sister and I weren't allowed to watch TV on weekdays. Whenever my mom caught us watching TV on a school day, she'd get really mad and shut it off.

I had issues with concentration and homework, so my mom did homework with me after school and in the evening, and if I had time left over, I practiced the flute or drew pictures. We watched a little TV on the weekends, but we didn't binge out on it. I thought the rules were kind of stupid. I think she believed that little kids might imitate the violence they saw on TV. To this day, I don't think I've ever seen an episode of *Power Rangers*.

When I was little, my dad would sort of try to be the nice guy and intervene to allow me to watch a bit of TV, but generally he fell in line with the guidelines my mom set down. As a family, we'd sit down on Saturday nights and watch a movie together, and that was fun. But my sister and I weren't allowed to watch whatever we wanted. And there wasn't any negotiation about finishing my homework and being allowed to watch on weeknights. It was a hard-and-fast rule in our house—no TV on weeknights.

Q: How did you feel about your parents' trying to control what programs you watched on TV?

Stefan: The consensus in my family was that violent material would affect me adversely, and material that was offensive, like *South Park*, would cause me to imitate it. And my mom didn't want me listening to violent or misogynistic rap music. There was this sense that negative gender stereotyping, violence, and gross behavior would affect children who watched it, and my parents tried to steer clear of it. They felt all this could affect me and influence me in a negative way.

In retrospect, I think that if I had been allowed to watch *South Park* as a child, I definitely would have imitated the gross language and snarky attitudes of the characters on that show. There was an awareness in my home that without restriction kids would just sit and watch TV endlessly and let the content just wash over them, and I think my mom saw that. I was a kid with a sponge-like brain, and she thought that I was "programmable" in a way and that material that was too sexual or violent or misogynistic would affect my thinking. When I got older, my parents and I would watch TV together and critique the commercials; there was a sense of awareness that TV was mainly trying to sell us things.

Q: Did your mom and dad control your use of the computer?

Sonja: AOL Instant Messenger (AIM) was new and very popular when I was in middle school, and I was on it constantly. I think my parents really struggled to regulate the amount of time I was allowed to IM with my friends. Their method of regulation was to shout up the back stairs at me, "Get off Instant Messenger!" But unless my parents were standing at the bottom of the stairs listening, they wouldn't know that I was IMing for hours at a time. And when they did yell up from the kitchen, I'd shout back, "Okay!" and I'd just keep IMing. I was a typical obnoxious teenager.

AIM was a huge time suck. It was just a waste of time. But at the time, AIM was the main portal to social life when we were growing up. I don't think my parents did what some frustrated parents did—log in to my AIM and see what I was messaging. They just shouted up the stairs at me. They seemed to trust me, and sometimes they'd just give up when I'd push back and whine about needing to stay in touch with my friends. But I certainly got the message that homework came first in our house. And I generally followed the rules.

The attraction for me of being able to instant message was being able to communicate with people I didn't see all the time. I went to an all-girl school, and I remember having fun conversations with boys over AIM. I never talked to kids outside of my friends' networks, so I wasn't communicating with strangers. It felt safe, and it was a way for me to get to know kids outside my school. We had dances at the school where they invited boys, but that was always a little awkward, so AIM was another way to get to know boys. It wasn't as formal or intrusive as a phone call. My brother and I shared a computer, and when I wanted to use AIM, I would use the excuse that I was older and had homework, so I could dominate and control the computer and keep my little brother off it. And I don't think he cared that much, because Stephan was never that attached to technology. He didn't care much for computer games or AIM. He was a reader and a musician. In high school, he was in a band, so he never got addicted to the internet or gaming. When he was little, he'd go out and ride his bike and play on his skateboard when he got home from school. He was lucky that on our block there were lots of kids his age, so he had friends close by to play with, and they didn't hole up inside in front of a computer. I was a little more attached to technology because I didn't have friends on my street.

Q: Did Facebook and other social media networks play a big part in your childhood?

Stefan: I'm not that attached to Facebook, so I don't waste a lot of time on it. In ninth and tenth grade, my friends cared a lot more about it. I remember kids worrying about how many photos they were in and how many Facebook friends they had. I was distracted by it sometimes, but social media was never my main focus. In hindsight, I know I've probably been on Facebook for hundreds of hours, and there's no doubt I could have made better use of that time, but I was doing other things like playing music and reading.

Sonja: In graduate school, Facebook and other social media is a huge problem in the classroom. Some professors allow laptops with the understanding that students are taking notes on a lecture. But kids will sit there with their laptops open, pretending to be taking notes, but you can see their screens. They're checking their Facebook, posting on Instagram, answering emails, writing papers for other classes. There's no way they can be absorbing what the professor is saying. And this isn't junior college; this is graduate school. I don't think I've ever been in a classroom in grad school where people weren't multitasking on their phones and laptops, and these are discussion-based classes, and people are on Facebook and not paying attention to the professor, so there are long, awkward moments of silence in the middle of a classroom discussion because people aren't paying attention; they aren't engaged. They're thinking, *Well, I'm not in love with this class, so I might as well check my email, or do some research on the web, or work on my job application.*

When I'm in class and I'm stressed out, I'll check my Facebook and watch for incoming texts and emails. Technology is a huge distraction. I don't think they should allow technology in the classroom. Students are really good at finding excuses to use technology. Stressed out? Got to check my Facebook. Don't have a date for the weekend? Got to send a text and check my email. When I look at my phone in class, it's either because I feel bored or I'm feeling anxious because I haven't heard from my boyfriend. But I'm not sure how wise that really is when you're paying top dollar to a graduate school and preparing for a career. We're paying to learn from people, not from technology.

Q: If you had children, would you feel it was necessary to regulate their use of electronic media?

Sonja: Kids are using technology in very different ways from when I was a child in the 1990s. Kids are using iPads for schoolwork now. And kids who use technology to do homework also use it for social media and games. I'm not sure how wise it is to give kids iPads to do their homework. They have access to games, they can go online, and use apps. I think it's a huge distraction. If I were a parent, I'd limit the use of technology to homework and allow a limited amount of fun time, like maybe a half hour a night after homework. Then I'd put the thing away.

I tutored a little boy when I was an undergraduate, and I limited the amount of time he could play on the computer because I thought it distracted him from people-building skills. And I limited the types of games he could play; I didn't allow him to play violent games. So I would limit time spent, and I would limit the content based on age appropriateness.

Q: What do you think about the ways in which people are using their cell phones?

Sonja: I have friends who will take a picture of any place they walk into whether it's lunch or buying underwear at JC Penney. And then they have to upload it to Instagram before they can have a conversation with you, and then there's the constant checking to see how many likes they have. I guess it's for social recognition. Ten years ago, maybe someone would bring a camera to a special occasion, but they wouldn't be on their phones constantly. Today, it's gotten a little weird.

When the iPhone first came out, people called it the conversation stopper. Now, I guess people are used to conversations stopping. With text messages, people expect you to respond instantly, and when you don't, they get hurt or stressed or worried. I think it harms your ability to be present in the social setting you're in. I get really annoyed when I look around and my friends are on their phones. Some people get frustrated with me because I won't respond to texts or calls when I'm with other people. I think it detracts from one-on-one time that people share.

Today, Peter and Bridget's son, Stefan, is an affable, bright, and thoughtful young man who has spent the last four years at a top eastern university designing his own college major which involves art history, music, film studies, politics, and the study of media. He calls his major "Visual Rhetoric." It is my belief that Stefan benefited greatly from the guidance and restrictions his parents placed upon electronic media in his house when he was growing up.

His sister, Sonja, is getting her MBA at a top Ivy League university. Sonja has strong opinions about how today's digital technology both helps and hinders young people. She is a resourceful, delightful young adult.

FAMILY #4: MY DAUGHTERS, MIRANDA AND ARIANNA

Ignoring my own fear of failure to adequately protect my own children from the side effects of too much technology, I interviewed my daughters. The answers I got were candid, heartening, and at times disconcerting, reminding me of the old saying, the cobbler's children have no shoes.

Miranda is a college sophomore studying art and education. Her older sister, Arianna, is a college drama graduate; she sells retail clothing and works as a voice actor.

Q: Do you recall what the rules were at home regarding watching TV when you were kids?

Miranda: The rule you guys set up when I was in elementary school was I wasn't allowed to watch TV on weekdays, and I was allowed to watch for only a few hours on weekends. But what really happened was, Sissy [her older sister, Arianna] would babysit for me when you and Mom would go out for a movie, and we would pig out on TV and videos. She and I negotiated about what to watch, because she was eight years older, and we wanted to watch different things. You didn't allow R-rated movies in the house, so we watched Disney videos, Muzzy, stuff like that. When you and Mom had been gone for over three hours, we knew you were probably on your way home from the movie, so we would lower the volume on the TV set and listen for the sound of your key in the door, and when we heard you coming in, we'd turn off the TV, hide the remote under the pillows on the couch, and pick up books and pretend we were reading.

(When my wife and I arrived home after a night out, I could usually tell that my kids had been watching TV. When we came in the door, the two of them would be squirming on the couch, looking nervous, pretending to read a book, and when I'd put my hand on the back of the TV set, it would be warm.)

Q: Do you remember what the restrictions were regarding media, and did it have an effect on you?

Arianna: I remember before I was a teenager I wasn't allowed to watch much TV except for *Pee Wee's Playhouse* with Pee Wee

Herman>; you and I watched that together on Saturday mornings. And I watched Gumby videos. I remember feeling a little left out at school sometimes because so many of my friends rushed home from school and sat for hours in front of the TV, and you guys wouldn't let me do that. One girl at school said, "You haven't seen the new *Teenage Mutant Ninja Turtles* episode?" And I thought, that's stupid. It was like, who cares? You took me to the *Teenage Mutant Ninja Turtles* movie, so I could at least talk about the characters with my friends.

In elementary school, I slept over at my friend Emily's a lot, and she had a TV in her room, and she was allowed to fall asleep in front of the TV every night. Her mom had hooked up an electric timer to the TV so that after Emily fell asleep, the timer would turn off the TV at midnight so it wouldn't stay on all night and waste electricity. Whenever I was at Emily's, I'd lie there all night glued to the TV, watching *I Love Lucy* reruns until the timer switched it off at midnight.

Even then, I remember thinking it was kind of sad that my friend needed the TV on in order to fall asleep. I'm lucky, because you read to me every night when I was a little girl, so today I use a book to fall asleep. Reading feels different. It's a comforting thing to read before I go to bed. It's a tradition you guys instilled in me. These days, I read three or four pages of something every night before I go to sleep.

Q: Do you remember trying to get around the rules?

Miranda: When Joanie [a seventy-year-old family friend] babysat for me, I manipulated her into letting me watch TV when you guys were out. But as I got older, TV became less of an interest of mine. It's interesting that you were a little stricter with my older sister before I was born, and today she watches more TV than I do, and she talks about TV—plotlines of series, the characters. I don't much care about it these days. When I'm home on vacation from college,

I'll make myself breakfast and turn on some dumb sitcom—*That 70's Show* or maybe an on-demand movie—but most of the time I'd rather be out jogging or interacting with friends than sitting in front of a TV set or my computer.

I remember we watched a few programs as a family, like *Gossip Girl* and *Friends*, and that was fun, like a family ritual, but you would turn it off after the episode, so we wouldn't sit and veg out for the entire evening. I remember you used to let me watch *That's So Raven* and *Lizzie McGuire*. TV was always something that you and Mom treated as a bit of a privilege when homework was done, and I had to be a little sneaky about watching more when you weren't around.

Q: Were each of you treated differently because of your age difference?

Arianna: I remember being jealous that my little sister got to watch more TV than I did when I was little. But you guys were careful with both of us on the issue of R-rated movies. And you wouldn't let us watch PG-13 movies until we were thirteen. I have a TV in the apartment I share with a roommate, but more often than not, it's like digital wallpaper. I'll have it on while I'm cleaning my room or eating supper, and I'll be checking my Facebook and texting at the same time, so if a TV show is brilliant, I'll have to watch the series over again to really understand it, since I multitask a lot when I'm watching and I miss the show. And I don't think we do any of the multitasks particularly well.

Q: Was there anything positive about being restricted from access to media at home?

Arianna: You raised us on movies more than TV. We watched movies as a family activity, so today, I prefer watching old movies more than television shows. We made movies a family event. We'd all sit down, turn the lights off, eat popcorn, and watch an old movie together. That's what I remember about watching television when

I was little. I love movies, and it's probably because you guys made movies a fun event. When I watch a movie at home, I make a cup of tea, light a candle, and sit in my bed and watch the movie.

And I appreciate the fact that you paid attention to movie ratings. I think kids are exposed to way too much way too early these days with cable TV and the internet. Kids need time to be kids and not be exposed to the horror and gore that passes for entertainment. Kids can find pornography with a simple keyword on Google. I'm afraid a whole generation of boys who watched internet pornography are going to have a very different set of expectations from girls than the pre-internet generation. Who knows what that's going to do to their dating prospects?

Q: Did you know why we tried to control your viewing habits?

Miranda: I've grown up with the saying, "TV melts your brain." Ever since I can remember, you would tell me that. And for a while I think I believed it literally, that if I watched too much TV my brain would slowly begin to melt and I would become really stupid.

Q: Did you think that was true when you were little?

Miranda: I still think it's true.

Q: Did you think it was silly that we made rules about watching TV?

Miranda: Yes, sometimes I found it frustrating. I wondered, *Why can't I watch more TV? Why can't I have a TV in my room?* However, even as a little girl, I knew there wasn't much that was educational or constructive about watching TV. But I had so many friends who had TVs in their rooms, and they could watch whenever they wanted, and I was sort of in awe of that. But I had an intuitive sense that there was something wrong with unlimited watching because you and Mom set rules in our house. I didn't think you guys were weird for not letting me watch it.

These days, as a college student, I find myself thinking that TV is a bit silly and a time suck. There are shows that are certainly entertaining, but when I hear about kids who watch a lot, I think it's sad and takes away from experiencing life and socializing with people. I've decided that when I have a family of my own, I won't even have a television in my home. I might want a TV monitor to watch movies and documentaries. I just feel that watching TV takes time away from you, precious time, and human interaction. And I get turned off by all the commercials. I find these days that the way I watch TV, like on vacation, is I'll just flick through channels, and I won't find anything very engaging, and I'll just turn it off because it bores me.

Q: Do you remember your first experiences with social media?

Arianna: I remember AOL Instant Messenger was a big deal when I was in middle-school. I would be IMing my friends instead of doing my homework. And I played this computer game for girls called *Rockett's New School*. I loved it. I played it a lot. When you or Mom would come in my room to check up on me on a school night, I'd just hide the game on my screen behind a Word document and pretend to be doing homework. Same thing with AOL Instant Messaging. I'd always have a homeworky-looking document ready to hide my IMing from you when you came in my room.

Q: What was your attitude about TV and electronic media when you were a child?

Miranda: In high school, I hung out with a group of kids who loved to hike and be outdoors. I was an art student, so a lot of my friends loved to draw, and a bunch of us hung out on weekends drawing pictures, shooting videos, talking with each other, and doing things outdoors. I surrounded myself with the kind of people who love interaction and collaboration and doing interesting things like going to the beach or attending friends' music shows. I was in this mindset as a teenager to really milk life for what it had to offer and not waste time. I really loved childhood, and I loved playing, and I found in high school that time was beginning to speed up; it was going by so fast, and I was growing up so fast that I felt, *I have to keep playing, I don't want to miss my childhood.* I wanted to get as much as I could from every moment, and I find that television and social media take away from that. And that's why even the idea of going to a movie makes me a little nervous, because I'd rather be interacting with people and not sitting, staring at a screen.

Q: Do you see any drawbacks to using social media?

Arianna: I have watched people have mental breakdowns on Facebook. I knew two college girls who posted about their mental deterioration. One wrote that she had done drugs, and she said it unleashed her latent bipolar disease. She started posting on friends' walls that she hated them, didn't trust them—people she hadn't seen in years. I log on to Facebook expecting to see photos of my friends' latest social activities, and instead I see someone's latest nervous breakdown.

This other girl decided that because of a breakup she hated men, and she sent hate messages to her male friends on Facebook. She tagged pictures of random guys she was friends with. Her crazy Facebook posts went on for days. I hadn't seen this girl in years, and yet I am getting an intimate portrait of her mental breakdown because she chose to put it on Facebook. I guess the moral of the story is, be careful before you hit "post."

Cell phones present a different problem. I don't think we've learned good cell phone etiquette yet. We need a digital version of Miss Manners. If I'm out for a nice dinner, I won't take my phone out. But if I'm just sitting around with a friend, we'll have our phones out, I'll Instagram, we'll be looking up something on my phone, and if I get a text, I'll answer it. I know it's rude, but that's because I'm over twenty-four years old.

Younger people have no idea how rude it is to be texting all the time. I wasn't raised with this kind of technology. Younger kids who are just starting college are so used to it; a smartphone is like an appendage. They think it's normal to be texting all the time. And with dating these days, it's rare to have a guy call you. He'll text. Friday night at ten o'clock, it's normal for a girl to get a text from some guy she hardly knows: "What're you up to?" And it's a turnoff. That's no way to get in touch with someone you're interested in. The kind of man I like will call and ask me out on a date. We might text information like time and place, but phone calls are the way to go in romance. But it's perfectly normal these days for dates to be arranged strictly by text, and you won't actually talk until you sit down for dinner with the person.

Miranda: My boyfriend and I get mad at each other when we go on our phones. He'll check his Instagram, then I'll go, "Okay, I'll check *my* Instagram," and suddenly there's this wall between us— this little pair of screens we're relating to. I'll think, *Oh, well he's on his phone, he won't care if I'm on my phone,* and then it turns into this little argument, "Oh, is that what we're doing now? How's Instagram?" Sometimes, when we're together, we make each other delete the Instagram app from our phones. Because once you start to care about spending time with someone, and they just randomly pick up their phone, it really bothers you. And when someone picks up their phone to read a text it becomes clear that they really don't know that anything else is going on in the room but their phone.

Talking directly with families reinforced my belief about the need for an open and candid dialogue between parents and children about electronic media and entertainment in the home. The challenges a family faces in today's digital world are monumental. But through patient discussion and by following your gut instincts, families can make it through. The manner in which you mediate your child's access to technology and the degree of success you will have will be a direct reflection of the nature of your emotional relationship with your child. If you have a relationship of mutual trust, then regulating your child's access to technology will be relatively pain free. But if your relationship with your child is untrusting, then controlling your child's behavior with digital technology will be a rockier road.

From adolescents involved in computer gaming to graduate students checking their Facebook and email in class—if the apps and software they use are addictive, then Houston, we have a problem. And if we can't teach our kids to control their impulse to check their screens repeatedly whether or not they're in the presence of friends or family, it would appear that we have an even bigger problem.

The emotional ramifications of trying to control children's behavior can be complex and difficult, but the choices a parent has regarding control of digital media in your home are relatively simple. Here is a list of suggestions and questions to consider:

- Start by explaining and discussing with your child why, when, and how you are going to control their access to their cell phone, television, video, iPad, game platform, and computer. Ask your child for suggestions. It will help them become part of the process.
- Decide where these devices should be in your home. Should there be a TV or a game platform in a child's bedroom? Should their computer be in their room or in a central location? Should they park their cell phone with you when they get home or when they're doing homework?
- Should you allow your child to have a smart phone or a traditional cell phone with no internet access?
- Should you enable texting on your child's phone?
- Should there be set hours for homework and set hours for recreational use of phones, other digital devices, gaming, and TV and video watching?

- How many computers, cell phones, television sets, video monitors, and digital recording devices (DVR) should your children have access to in your home?
- Should you have scheduled family time in front of the TV?
- Do you read to your child every night?

Education writer Dana Goldstein reported in the April 14, 2014 edition of *The Atlantic* that professors from University of Texas and Duke did an extensive study of parent-child relations and academic achievement with an eye on what kind of parental involvement works and what doesn't. They found that, of the dozens of ways parents try to influence their children, the three most important things a parent can do to affect academic success are:

1. Read aloud to your children (fewer than half of American parents do).
2. Talk with your children about the long-range ramifications of getting good grades and the value and appeal of continued education.
3. Get your child placed in a classroom with a teacher with a good reputation. (Studies show the best teachers raise students' lifetime earnings and decrease the likelihood of teen pregnancy.)

Navigating the waters of parenthood is an exhilarating, sometimes trying, often exhausting, and hopefully deeply gratifying part of life. Sharing your travels with other families is one of the most helpful things you can do. It gives you perspective on your own joys and tribulations. I learned a lot just listening to other parents and their kids about their family journey.

CONCLUSION

Young people have been drawn into a world of intense digital connectedness, and barring blackouts and internet crashes, there appears to be no way out. Aside from the convenience, fun, and the "wow" factor, there is no convincing evidence that this level of digital connection is a positive thing.

The PBS news program *Frontline* went to the Massachusetts Institute of Technology (MIT) to find out how the best and brightest of American college students are doing now that they are wired up to the internet. Most MIT professors allow laptops in the classroom for note taking. Some don't allow laptops because they know that students are doing more than taking notes; they're texting, checking Facebook, etc.

MIT Associate Professor David Jones says you can test today's wired students on two sorts of things: "You can tell how well they're paying attention in lecture, and you can test how well they're absorbing information from assigned readings. And I don't think they're doing either of those things well."

Professor Mark Bauerlein of Emory University says, "You will find a lot of English professors saying, 'I can't assign a novel of more than two hundred pages. I used to. I can't anymore.'" MIT student, Brian, admits, "I'm pretty much constantly texting. And whenever I study, I'm watching a YouTube video, I'm checking my email nonstop, refreshing the page, you know, on Facebook, Facebook Chat . . . so that I can always stay connected."

Brian is the typical post-modern multitasker. He thinks he's good at it. But MIT Professor Clifford Nass believes otherwise. "Virtually all multitaskers think they're brilliant at multitasking. . . . It turns out multitaskers are terrible at every aspect of multitasking. They get distracted constantly; their memory is very disorganized. Recent work we've done suggests they're worse at analytic reasoning. We worry that it may be creating people who are unable to think well or clearly."[33]

Reports from other parts of the world are equally grim. In South Korea, 90 percent of Korean children use the internet in daily life. Korean healthcare experts are now treating internet addiction as a psychiatric disorder.

Schools are becoming progressively more and more wired. Jason Levy is the principal of I.S. 399, a middle school in South Bronx, New York, that experienced a positive turnaround with the introduction of internet technology to the classroom.

Levy says, "To me, there should never be a question as to whether or not students should have access to technology. Technology is like oxygen, and no one would ever have an argument that we should take away oxygen from the kids. I think, if anything, we make school make more sense for them when we provide them with the opportunity to use technology."

Daniel Ackerman, Assistant Principal of I.S. 399, spends a portion of his day monitoring what students are doing online. "A student has the photo booth program open. He's got his social studies project open, school email open. . . . What I see a lot of is multitasking."[34]

Todd Oppenheimer, author of the book *The Flickering Mind*, says, "My concern with digital media is that it's such short attention span stuff . . . It's what I call 'instant gratification education.' A thought comes to you, you pursue it. You see a website, you click on it. You want to hear music while you're studying, you do it. All this bifurcates the brain, keeps it from being able to pursue one linear thought, and teaches you that you should be able to have every urge answered the minute the urge occurs."[35]

The truth be told, I like my tech world. I like the convenience. I like the ritual. Okay, I don't *love* turning on my computer in the morning, I just like what it does for me. And when it fails, I have my iPhone, which has saved me on numerous occasions. I even like my new "Smart TV" (I'm not sure what's so "smart" about it, except that it's large and wired to the internet). My iPad sits in my voiceover booth and saves me from wasting paper. But I never take my iPad out of the booth. I just don't relish being online 24/7. When my older daughter comes down to my studio to audition for a cartoon voice job, she uses my iPad, and I always fear that she'll say, "Wow, an iPad. Can I borrow it, dad?" But she never has. She doesn't own one. She uses a laptop. I'm happy she doesn't crave another digital device in her life.

Most of the time, my electronic screens serve me well. I like them. I've always liked technology. I like receiving texts from my daughter at college. I even text her those ridiculous little smiley emoticons. Sometimes we FaceTime each other with our iPhones. We group text when we want to include my wife and my older daughter. I send them all links to my favorite websites. I even have an Instagram account where I enjoy fussing with my photos and showing them to friends in my iPhone. I take "selfies" of me and my family with my cell phone camera. They're never perfect, but they're fun, and they please the folks we send them to. I like the fact that I can stay connected to my family and do most of my work myself with the aid of this amazing stuff.

When our kids were little, we took some control over their personal electronics, and we limited their screen time. When they got older, we experimented with website blocks on their computers—an awkward and not altogether successful effort. And I downloaded Life360, a child-tracking smartphone app, which I surreptitiously installed on my younger daughter's phone when she was in high school. When I fired it up on my phone and showed it to my wife, she was amazed.

"You mean we know where she is at all times?"

"I guess." I stared at my phone, scratched my head, and wondered how this was going to benefit us. I felt like an intelligence operative, albeit an inexperienced one. My wife and I swore an oath of silence.

"We can never tell Miranda," I warned her. On Saturday nights we stared at my phone and watched the tiny red dot that represented our daughter, or at least our daughter's cell phone, inch its way along freeways. It would stop mysteriously in a neighborhood we weren't familiar with.

"Where is she?" my wife would ask.

"Right here. She's the red dot."

When my daughter's cellphone reception weakened, the red dot disappeared.

"What happened to her?" my wife would ask. "Where did she go?"

"Cell reception must be bad. She's in the hills."

"But she hasn't moved. Should we call her?"

And occasionally we did. But teenagers are apt to send a cell phone call to voicemail. They prefer texting. Usually, we got her voicemail.

I soured on this child-tracking app when it began sending me alerts that there were convicted sex offenders in the neighborhood. I always wondered how they knew a sex offender was near; it was creepy, and it seemed irrelevant to our lives. When our daughter graduated high school and upgraded her phone, we gave up on cellular child tracking.

Spyware notwithstanding, all in all, our home has been a safe, happy, creative place for our kids to grow up in. They got into good colleges. I still give them advice when needed, and we celebrate the good times together.

I remember watching my daughter at age four hold a TV remote in her hand for the first time. Now, she's twenty-seven. She hates it when I hold the remote. "Dad, give me the remote!" We had a fight in front of friends while we were watching the Academy Awards. I paused the TV so I could comment to everyone about how the Academy votes, or at least how I think they vote.

"Dad, people don't want to hear this. Give me the remote."

"No. This is my house, and this is my remote."

There were friends in the room, two of whom were psychotherapists. Afterwards, one of them said, "She was really out of line."

The other one said, "You two have some issues to work out."

It seems that navigating power issues around technology with your children never really stops, even after they've grown up.

In our tech lives, each member of our family has their own private rhythms and rituals. And the roles have occasionally reversed. Our kids grew up with new media, and they have a more refined set of skills with technology than their parents. Our children are faster with electronics, more sure of themselves—like agile, well-practiced cyborgs.

I'm not anti-technology. But just as I refused to buy my children new cars for high school graduation (good decision, since the inevitable did happen—both my children banged up their used cars), I also refused to give my children free rein with personal electronics. There were more than a few teary-eyed nights when I walked out of their bedrooms with their cellphones in my hand and stashed them in my sock drawer for the night. There were more than a few visits from our computer tech solely for the purpose of blocking websites and restricting our children's access to the internet. We refused to allow gaming platforms in the house. There were many nights when I grabbed the TV remote out of their hands and hit the "off" button, and their whines of protest could be heard by neighbors down the street.

For me, the most difficult part of parenting has been enduring the pushback from our kids when we laid down the law. But childrearing is what I signed up for. And it has been the most rewarding, most loving, most powerful life experience I could ever dream of having.

I hope you've enjoyed the stories and the simple prescriptions offered here for managing your family's digital devices and electronic media in your home. Remember, the most important principles of parenting apply in every age—not just this digital one. Maintain open communication, set and stick to appropriate limits, read to your kids, talk about their future, find them the best teachers you can, and tell your children you love them.

I wish you the best of luck.

SOURCES

1. Gary Small. *iBrain: Surviving the Technological Alteration of the Modern Mind.* New York: HarperCollins. 2009.

2. Shelley Peck. "Hitting the Off Button: How Parents Can Stand Up for Less Screen Time at Home." National PTA. pta.org/programs/content. cfm?ItemNumber=999.

3. Janet Kornblum. "Study: More Parents Use TV as an Electronic Babysitter." *USA Today.* 2006. usatoday30.usatoday.com/tech/news/2006-05-24-kids-media_x.htm.

4. Newton N. Minow. "Newton Minow Interview." Archive of American Television. 1999. http://emmytvlegends.org/interviews/people/newton-n-minow.

5. Tony Dokoupil. "Is the Internet Making Us Crazy? What the New Research Says." *Newweek.* 2012. http://www.newsweek.com/internet-making-us-crazy-what-new-research-says-65593.

6. KidsHealth.com. "How TV Affects Your Child." KidsHealth. 2011. kidshealth.org/parent/positive/family/tv_affects_child.html.

7. Ann Vorisek White. "Breaking Out of the Box: Turn Off TV, Turn on Life." Mothering 1 July 2001: 70-76.

8. Daniel Goleman. "How Viewers Grow Addicted to Television." *The New York Times.* 1990. nytimes.com/1990/10/16/science/how-viewers-grow-addicted-to-television.html?pagewanted=all&src=pm.

9. Kurtis Hiatt. "Fast Food Restaurants Increase Ads Aimed at Kids." *US News.* 2010. http://health.usnews.com/health-news/diet-fitness/diet/

articles/2010/11/08/health-buzz-fast-food-restaurants-increase-ads-aimed-at-kids.

10. Harvard School of Public Health. "Television Watching and 'Sit Time.'" Harvard School of Public Health. http://www.hsph.harvard.edu/obesity-prevention-source/obesity-causes/television-and-sedentary-behavior-and-obesity/

11. Wikipedia. "Hasbro." Wikipedia. 2014. http://en.wikipedia.org/wiki/Hasbro.

12. Medline Plus. "Television Watching." Medline Plus. 2014. http://www.nlm.nih.gov/medlineplus/ency/article/002329.htm.

13. American Psychological Association. "Violence on Television: What Do Children Learn? What Can Parents Do?" American Psychological Association. 1999. http://www.cmu.edu/CSR/case_studies/tv_violence.html.

14. Sarah Harris. "Young Children Believe TV Images Are Real." MailOnline.com. 2006. http://www.dailymail.co.uk/news/article-404267/Young-children-believe-TV-images-real.html.

15. Bill Goodwin. "The Undeniable Influence of Kids." *Packaging Digest*. 2013. http://www.packagingdigest.com/packaging-design/undeniable-influence-kids

16. Children's Ministry Magazine. "What You Can Learn from Sesame Street." *Children's Ministry Magazine*. 2012. http://childrensministry.com/articles/what-you-can-learn-from-sesame-street/.

17. Andrea Chang. " YouTube's Biggest Stars Are Cashing In Offline." *Los Angeles Times*. 2014. http://www.latimes.com/business/la-fi-youtube-stars-20140808-story.html#page=1.

18. Rachel Dretzin. "Transcript: Digital Nation." PBS Frontline. Quoting Douglas Rushkoff. 2010. http://www.pbs.org/wgbh/pages/frontline/digitalnation/etc/script.html.

19. Max von Boehn. *Dolls*. New York:Dover Books. 1972

20. The Economist. "Retail Theory: How Ernest Dichter, an acolyte of Sigmund Freud, Revolutionized Marketing." 2011. http://www.economist.com/node/21541706.

21. Tanya Lee Stone. *The Good, the Bad, and the Barbie*. New York: Viking Press. 2010.

22. Local News. "The Ratings Game." PBS. http://www.pbs.org/wnet/insidelocalnews/ratings.html.

23. Lenore Skenazy. *Free-Range Kids*. San Fransisco: Jossey-Bass. 2009.

24. Steven Pinker. *The Better Angels of Our Nature: Why Violence Has De-clined*. New York: Penguin Books. 2012.

25. Tamar Lewin. "If Your Kids Are Awake, They're Probably Online." *The New York Times*. 2010. http://www.nytimes.com/2010/01/20/education/20wired.html?_r=0.

26. Sarah Lyall. "The Case of the Accidental Superstar." *New York Times' Style Magazine*. 2014. http://tmagazine.blogs.nytimes.com/2014/03/07/the-case-of-the-accidental-superstar/?_php=true&_type=blogs&_r=0.

27. Joseph Campbell. *Power of Myth*. New York: First Anchor Books. 1991.

28. De Botton, Alain. *The News: A User's Manual*. New York: Pantheon Books. 2014.

29. Eckhart Tolle. *The Power of Now*. Vancouver, Canada: Namaste Publishing. 1997.

30. Rachel Dretzin. "Transcript: Digital Nation." PBS Frontline. 2010. http://www.pbs.org/wgbh/pages/frontline/digitalnation/etc/script.html.

31. Barbara J. Wilson. "Media and Children's Aggression, Fear, and Altruism." The Future of Children. 2008. http://futureofchildren.org/publications/journals/article/index.xml?journalid=32&articleid=58.

32. James Rainey. "The Moth Gives Wings to Young Storytellers." Participant Media. 2011. http://www.participantmedia.com/2011/08/moth-wings-young-storytellers/.

33. PBS Frontline. "What Is Multitasking." PBS Frontline. 2010. http://www.pbs.org/wgbh/pages/frontline/digitalnation/interviews/nass.html.

34. Rachel Dretzin. "Transcript: Digital Nation." PBS Frontline. Quoting Daniel Ackerman. 2010. http://www.pbs.org/wgbh/pages/frontline/digitalnation/etc/script.html.

35. Todd Oppenheimer. *The Flickering Mind: Saving Education from the False Promise of Technology*. New York: Random House. 2004.

ABOUT THE AUTHOR

Bill Ratner is one of America's most popular voiceover artists on movie trailers, computer games, commercials, TV programs, and documentaries. He is the original voice of "Flint" in the *G.I. Joe* TV cartoon. His spoken word performances are featured on National Public Radio's *Good Food* and *The Business*. He is a nine-time winner of The Moth Story Slams, a published essayist, short story writer, public speaker, parent, and educator. He founded *TV Cartoon Scandals: Media Awareness for Children*® for the Los Angeles Unified School District in 1992. He has taught and performed at the Screen Actors Guild Foundation, League for the Advancement of New England Storytelling, Windsor Mountain International, Timpanogos Storytelling Conference, Northlands Storytelling Conference, and the National Storytelling Festival.

More information can be found at www.billratner.com.

ABOUT FAMILIUS

Welcome to a place where mothers are celebrated, not compared. Where heart is at the center of our families, and family at the center of our homes. Where boo boos are still kissed, cake beaters are still licked, and mistakes are still okay. Welcome to a place where books—and family—are beautiful. Familius: a book publisher dedicated to helping families be happy.

VISIT OUR WEBSITE: WWW.FAMILIUS.COM

Our website is a different kind of place. Get inspired, read articles, discover books, watch videos, connect with our family experts, download books and apps and audiobooks, and along the way, discover how values and happy family life go together.

JOIN OUR FAMILY

There are lots of ways to connect with us! Subscribe to our newsletters at www.familius.com to receive uplifting daily inspiration, essays from our Pater Familius, a free ebook every month, and the first word on special discounts and Familius news.

BECOME AN EXPERT

Familius authors and other established writers interested in helping families be happy are invited to join our family and contribute online content. If you have something important to say on the family, join our expert community by applying at:

www.familius.com/apply-to-become-a-familius-expert

GET BULK DISCOUNTS

If you feel a few friends and family might benefit from what you've read, let us know and we'll be happy to provide you with quantity discounts. Simply email us at specialorders@familius.com.

Website: www.familius.com

Facebook: www.facebook.com/paterfamilius

Twitter: @familiustalk, @paterfamilius1

Pinterest: www.pinterest.com/familius

The most important work

you ever do will be within the

walls of your own home.

CPSIA information can be obtained at www.ICGtesting.com
Printed in the USA
BVOW07s1618021014

369243BV00003B/3/P